The Little Helper Paradox

The Little Helper Paradox

LLM Between Promise and Responsibility

Michael Schmid

it-dialog e.K., Stuttgart

1st Edition 2026

ISBN 978-3-96459-031-2 (Paperback)
ISBN 978-3-96459-032-9 (Kindle)

Typeset based on a template by Johann-Christian Hanke. Set in Amazon Endure.

The contents of this book are intended for general orientation. They do not replace legal advice or professional review in individual cases.

AI Transparency: This book was written with the assistance of Claude (Anthropic). The author retains full editorial responsibility for all content. Details on the collaboration process can be found in Appendix "How This Book Was Created."

Table of Contents

Foreword

This book was born from discomfort.

I have worked in IT for over 43 years. I have witnessed mainframes, client-server architectures, the birth of the web, the cloud, and many more. Each wave brought promises. Some were kept. Many were not.

The current wave is called "Artificial Intelligence." More precisely: Large Language Models. Even more precisely: The idea that these systems can be used as a managed service for critical applications.

This idea worries me.

Why This Book

In January 2026, I published "Understanding Managed Services" (*Managed Services richtig verstehen*). The book explains how IT service contracts work—and how they often fail. The core message: A good contract requires measurable performance, clear responsibilities, and honest expectations.

I have been observing the LLM wave since 2023. Daily, I study the discussions and offerings on LinkedIn. I see the promises. I see the euphoria. And I see the same mistakes repeated that I have known for decades being, but this time, only worse.

Running my own LLM infrastructure would be the simplest solution—but for security reasons, also the most expensive. Appendix F shows the numbers: Anyone who truly wants to protect their data quickly ends up with six-figure amounts. That is not feasible for a mid-sized company like mine. So, I share the dilemma this book describes.

Providers promised "intelligent document analysis" and "AI-powered quality assurance." Customers believed they could delegate responsibility. Contracts were signed that no one can fulfill.

The problem is structural. A Large Language Model produces stochastic outputs. There is no guarantee of correctness. There is no way to guarantee correctness. This is not a bug—it is the principle.

A managed service for stochastic systems is an oxymoron. You can guarantee availability. You can guarantee response times. You cannot guarantee that the answers are correct.

I call this the Little Helper Paradox: The more you trust the system, the less you can verify the results. And the less you verify, the more dangerous the trust becomes.

Who This Book Is For

This book is for decision-makers facing the question: Should we deploy AI? And if so: how?

It is for engineers who want to understand what exactly they are supposed to use and what responsibility remains with them.

It is for lawyers and compliance officers who need to know what gaps exist in the regulatory framework.

It is for everyone who has the feeling that something is wrong with the promises, and who wants to understand why.

What This Book Is Not

This book is not a plea against Artificial Intelligence. LLMs are impressive tools. They can help with research, generate ideas, create drafts. I use them myself—daily.

This book is a plea for honesty. For realistic expectations. For knowing what works and what does not.

The message is not: "Don't use AI." The message is: "Understand what you are doing."

The Drone Example

Throughout this book runs one example: A company develops drone swarms. 2,000 pages of specification. An LLM is supposed to help find contradictions.

The example is not chosen randomly. As a trained telecommunications technician, I am interested in the drone problem for a specific reason: the radio bands. They are limited. They cannot be arbitrarily expanded. When hundreds of drones in a swarm must communicate in real-time, reliably, and without collision, latency becomes critical. Every millisecond counts. Every contradiction in the specification can lead to a crash.

The example is fictional. The problems are real.

Drones are a good example because errors there have consequences. A wrong latency specification does not lead to a typo in a report. It leads to a drone that crashes.

This makes the question urgent: Can you trust a system that sometimes lies—plausibly, but falsely?

Acknowledgments

This book has an unusual co-author: Claude, a Large Language Model from Anthropic.

This is not a marketing gimmick. Claude helped with structuring, sharpened arguments, provided counterarguments, suggested formulations. We discussed—about liability, about insurability, about the limits of systems like Claude itself.

I am aware of the irony: A book about the limits of LLMs, written with the help of an LLM.

But that is exactly the point. Claude was an excellent researcher and sparring partner. A critical proofreader. A tool that saved me work.

What Claude was not: A substitute for my own judgment. I verified every statement in this book. I drew every conclusion myself. The responsibility for the content lies with me—not with a language model.

That is exactly the division of labor this book recommends.

My thanks also go to the many conversation partners from the IT industry who shared their experiences with me—often on the condition of not being named. Their stories of failed projects, impossible contracts, and quiet unease have shaped this book.

Finally, I thank my partner for her patience with an author who sits at his desk in the evenings, discussing the limits of AI with an AI.

A Personal Note

I am not a lawyer. The legal analyses in this book are my assessment as an IT professional with decades of contract experience. They do not replace legal advice.

I am not an insurance broker. The statements about insurability are based on my research and conversations with industry experts. They do not replace advice from a specialist.

What I am: A practitioner who has seen too many projects fail. Who has read too many contracts that did not deliver what they promised. Who believes that honesty is the best protection—even when it is uncomfortable.

This book is my attempt to contribute that honesty.

Stuttgart, January 2026

Michael Schmid

The Question This Book Asks

A mid-sized company develops drone swarms. The specification comprises 2,000 pages. Dozens of engineers work on subsystems that must fit together in the end.

A service provider offers: “We analyze your documents with AI. Our system finds contradictions that humans overlook.”

That sounds good. That sounds like a solution.

The question this book asks: **Does it work?**

Not: Is the technology impressive? (Yes.) Not: Can it help with some tasks? (Yes.) But rather: Can a managed service for AI-powered document analysis be designed to work reliably for critical applications?

The answer this book reaches: **No. Structurally not.**

The Thesis

The central thesis can be stated in one sentence:

> Large Language Models cannot be operated as a managed service for critical applications because their core performance—content correctness—can neither be guaranteed, nor measured, nor contractually assured.

This is not a criticism of the technology. It is an analysis of the structure.

A managed service works like this: The provider promises a measurable performance. The customer pays for it. If the performance is not delivered, there are consequences.

With traditional IT, this works:

- Availability: measurable
- Response time: measurable
- Throughput: measurable

With an LLM, this does not work:

- Correctness: not measurable (without domain expertise)
- Completeness: not measurable (without knowing all documents)
- Reliability: not definable (with stochastic systems)

The provider can guarantee infrastructure. He cannot guarantee that the answers are correct.

The Little Helper Paradox

The book is named after a paradox that lies at the core of the problem.

An LLM is supposed to help. It is supposed to take work off the engineer's hands. It is supposed to find things he would overlook.

But:

> The more the system helps, the less the human verifies.

If the system finds 95% of the contradictions, why would the engineer still search himself? If the system cites a source, why would he look it up?

This is human. This is understandable. And this is dangerous.

Because the system does not find 95%. It sometimes finds 95%, sometimes 60%, sometimes 40%. It does not know how much it finds. It cannot say: "Warning, today I am unreliable."

The more the human trusts the system, the less he can evaluate the results.

This is the Little Helper Paradox: The system that is supposed to make work easier undermines the ability to control its work.

Why Drones?

The drone example runs through the entire book. This is not a coincidence.

First: Drones are complex. Hundreds of subsystems must work together. The documentation is extensive. The sources of error are manifold.

Second: Drones are critical. An error in the specification does not lead to a typo in a report. It leads to a drone that crashes. The consequences are real.

Third: Drones illustrate the latency problem. In a swarm, drones must communicate in real-time. Milliseconds count. If one specification says "50 ms maximum latency" and another says "325 ms measured under load," that is a critical contradiction. Exactly such contradictions the LLM is supposed to find.

Fourth: The technology is fascinating—but the physics is unforgiving. Radio bands are limited. Latencies are real. No AI can suspend the laws of electromagnetism.

The example is fictional. The problems are real. In every industry where errors have consequences.

Structure of the Book

The book is divided into four parts.

Part 1: The Promise (Chapters 1–4)

Part 1 describes what is promised—and why the promise is attractive.

- **Chapter 1** defines terms: What is AI? What is an LLM? What is a managed service?
- **Chapter 2** analyzes the promise for drone development: intelligent document analysis, automatic contradiction detection.
- **Chapter 3** examines local LLMs as an alternative: What do they solve? What still requires human effort?
- **Chapter 4** introduces the Little Helper Paradox: the core metaphor of the book.

Part 2: The Falsification (Chapters 5–8)

Part 2 attempts to keep the promise—and fails systematically.

The method is simple: **Try to write the contract.** If you cannot write a contract that protects both sides, the business model does not work.

- **Chapter 5** attempts to formulate an Service Level Agreement for LLM quality. It does not succeed.
- **Chapter 6** analyzes why wrong answers are not a bug but a *feature* of the architecture.
- **Chapter 7** asks who can validate the results—and arrives at uncomfortable answers.
- **Chapter 8** shows the managed service dilemma: The provider cannot see the data. He cannot assess the quality.

Part 3: The Consequences (Chapters 9–11)

Part 3 asks: What does this mean legally? Who is liable? Who bears the risk?

- **Chapter 9** analyzes the legal situation: German Civil Code (BGB), AI Act, Product Liability Directive—and their gaps. Additionally: The CLOUD Act and the question of which law your data is actually subject to.
- **Chapter 10** plays through the damage scenario: The drone crashes. Who is liable? No one clearly.
- **Chapter 11** examines insurability. Result: The core risk is not insurable.

Part 4: What Could Work (Chapters 12–16)

Part 4 is constructive. If managed service does not work—what then?

- **Chapter 12** proposes the Researcher Model: LLM as tool, not as decision-maker.
- **Chapter 13** describes organizational prerequisites: What must be in place before you start?
- **Chapter 14** discusses version pinning: Control instead of dependency.
- **Chapter 15** shows what can sensibly be agreed in SLAs—and what cannot.
- **Chapter 16** gives guidance for decision-makers: Questions, red flags, checklists.

What This Book Is Not

Not an anti-AI book. LLMs are impressive tools. They can be useful. This book itself uses an LLM—Claude from Anthropic—as a sparring partner and researcher.

Not a legal opinion. The legal analyses are the assessment of an IT practitioner, not a lawyer. They do not replace legal advice.

Not an implementation guide. The book does not describe how to technically set up an LLM. There are better sources for that.

Not alarmism. The world is not ending because LLMs exist. But it is becoming more complicated. This book attempts to describe part of that complexity.

What This Book Is

A plea for honesty.

The technology is impressive. The promises are often exaggerated. The contracts are often incomplete. The risks are often underestimated.

Those who know this can make better decisions.

Those who ignore this will sooner or later pay the price.

How to Read This Book

Linearly: From front to back. The argument builds on itself.

Selectively:

- For decision-makers: Chapter 4 (Paradox), Chapter 11 (Insurance), Chapter 16 (Guidance)
- For lawyers: Chapter 9 (Law), Chapter 10 (Liability)

- For engineers: Chapters 5–7 (SLA, Errors, Validation), Chapter 12 (Researcher Model)
- For everyone: Chapter 4 (Understanding the Paradox)

As a reference work: The glossary explains terms. The bibliography leads further. The key points at the end of each chapter summarize.

An Invitation

This book is an invitation to critical thinking.

Not: "Believe me." But rather: "Verify yourself."

If the arguments do not convince, object. If the examples do not fit, find better ones. If the conclusions are wrong, correct them.

That would be entirely in the spirit of the book: Do not trust blindly. Instead, verify, evaluate, decide.

Exactly what one should do with LLM outputs as well.

Stuttgart, January 2026

Part 1: The Promise

Chapter 1: What “Managed Service” Means—And What It Does Not

1.1 Classical Definition: Transfer of Responsibility to the Service Provider

A managed service is a contract about responsibility.

The provider takes over the operation of a system. He handles availability, maintenance, updates, troubleshooting. The customer pays a monthly flat rate and does not have to worry about anything.

That sounds simple. And it is—when certain conditions are met.

First: The provider must be able to see the system. He needs access to logs, configurations, error messages. Without insight, there is no responsibility.

Second: The provider must understand the system. He needs expertise for exactly this technology. Without competence, there is no problem-solving.

Third: The provider must be able to intervene. He needs authorization to make changes. Without the ability to act, no maintenance is possible.

Fourth: The performance must be measurable. Both sides must be able to verify whether the contract is being fulfilled. Without measurability, no contract can be fulfilled.

These four conditions form the foundation. If one is missing, “managed service” is just a combination of words.

1.2 Taxi, Rental Car, Own Car

A comparison from everyday life makes the differences tangible.

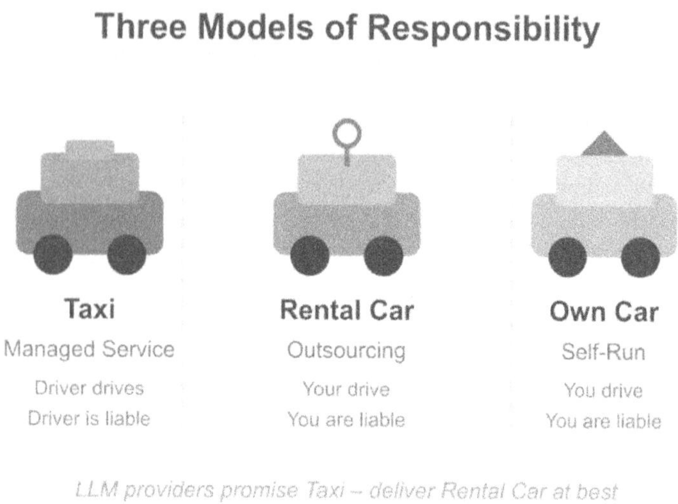

Figure 1 Three Models of Responsibility – Taxi, Rental Car, Own Car

The Taxi: Managed Service

You get in, name your destination, and lean back. The driver knows the way. She knows the traffic rules. She is insured. You pay at the end and get out.

This is managed service in its purest form. You delegate everything: vehicle, driver, knowledge, responsibility. The driver is liable for the route. You are only liable for the bill.

The Rental Car: Operations Outsourcing

You pick up the car. It is maintained, fueled, insured. But you drive yourself. You decide on the route. You are responsible for accidents.

This is the outsourcing of operations. The infrastructure is provided. The use remains with you. The rental company is liable for the condition of the vehicle. You are liable for what you do with it.

Your Own Car: In-House Operations

You buy the car. You maintain it. You fuel it. You drive it. Everything is up to you.

This is in-house operations. Maximum control. Maximum responsibility. Maximum effort.

The crucial question:

For an LLM for critical applications—which of these is possible?

Model	Who drives?	Who is liable for the route?
Taxi (Managed Service)	Driver	Driver
Rental Car (Outsourcing)	You	You
Own Car (In-House)	You	You

The managed service provider promises the taxi model. But with an LLM, he cannot drive. He does not know what you know. He does not understand your area. He cannot assess whether the answer is correct.

What he delivers is, at best, a rental car: functioning infrastructure. Driving—and being liable—you must do yourself.

1.3 The Managed Service Contract for Your Air Conditioning vs. for an LLM

Another comparison deepens the problem.

The Air Conditioning Example:

You sign a maintenance contract. The technician comes twice a year, checks the unit, replaces filters, measures performance. If the system fails, you call. Within 24 hours, someone is there.

The contract works because:

- The technician can see and touch the unit
- Air conditioning systems are standardized—the technician knows the model
- Performance is measurable: Does it condition the air or does it not?
- The technician can replace parts and change settings

The Large Language Model:

A provider promises: "We operate your LLM as a managed service. We take care of everything."

But what does "everything" mean?

Aspect	Air Conditioning	LLM
Access	Technician enters building	Provider may not see training data
Standardization	Known model	Individually trained model
Measurability	Measure temperature	Measure correctness?
Intervention	Replace spare part	What do you replace for hallucination?

The managed service provider can maintain the infrastructure. He can maintain servers, install updates, and guarantee availability.

He cannot guarantee that the answers are correct.

That is the crucial difference. With air conditioning, the core performance is measurable: air gets cooler. With an LLM, the core performance—content correctness—is not measurable. At least not by the provider.

1.4 Case Study Control Center: When Managed Service Is Just a Compilation of Words

Let’s imagine an energy utility that operates critical infrastructure. The control center monitors the grid. The system must function around the clock.

The company signs a managed service contract with an IT service provider. The contract states: 99.9% availability. 4-hour response time for incidents. 24/7 support.

That sounds like security. Reality, however, looks different.

Problem 1: Access

The control center processes sensitive data. The service provider is not allowed to see everything. For some incidents, he lacks the insight to find the cause. He reports: “From our perspective, everything is working.” The customer’s reality, on the other hand, is simple: It is *not* working.

Problem 2: Competence

The system has increased in scale over years. Hundreds of customizations, interfaces to legacy systems, special solutions. The service provider knows the standard product. He does not know the specific installation requirements. For complex incidents, the customer is left to his own devices.

Problem 3: Responsibility

Who is at fault when the system fails? The service provider points to a change the customer made. The customer points to inadequate maintenance. The contract does not help. It dictates availability, not causes.

The result:

After three years, the customer has a managed service contract—but his own team is conducting most of the work. The contract costs money. The security, however, is not delivered.

This is not criticism of the service provider. This is an analysis of the structure. Managed service works when the four conditions are met. For complex, individual, safety-critical systems, they often are not.

1.5 Key Points

- **Managed service is a contract about responsibility.** The provider takes over operations, maintenance, and problem resolution.
- **Four conditions must be met:** Access, competence, ability to act, measurability. If one is missing, the contract is worthless.
- **The taxi model only works if the driver can drive.** With LLMs, the provider lacks knowledge about your documents and your domain. At best, he delivers a rental car.
- **For air conditioning, the model works.** The core performance—cooling—is measurable. The technician can intervene.
- **For LLMs, the model does not work.** The core performance—content correctness—is not measurable. The provider can provide and maintain the infrastructure but cannot guarantee output quality.
- **"Managed service" often becomes an empty phrase.** For complex, individual systems, the real problems still remain the responsibility of the customer.

The question is not: Can LLMs be operated? The question is: Can responsibility for their accuracy be delegated? Chapter 2 shows why companies nevertheless believe they need exactly that.

Figure 2 Four Conditions for a Functioning Managed Service

Chapter 2: Why AI-as-a-Service?

2.1 AI Approaches at a Glance—Without Marketing Language

Before we talk about "AI as a Managed Service," we need to clarify what we are talking about. The term "Artificial Intelligence" is used liberally. From spam filters to self-driving cars, this use of the term is about as precise as "vehicle" for kick scooters and container ships.

Four approaches dominate the history of AI. They differ fundamentally—not only in technology but in what can be expected of them.

2.1.1 Four Generations of AI

Rule-Based Systems (1970s–1990s)

A subject matter expert formulates rules. A programmer codes them. The system executes them.

IF Temperature > 100°C AND Pressure > 10 bar THEN Issue warning

That works. As long as the world fits the rules.

Strength: Transparent. Traceable. Every decision is explainable.

Weakness: Rigid. A thousand rules for a thousand cases. The thousand-and-first case? Tough luck.

Rule-based systems still control production facilities today. They fail at anything that cannot be pressed into IF-THEN logic.

Caution: What engineers call "rule-based" could already be an "AI System" under the EU AI Act. The technical and legal definitions are not congruent. A simple spam filter can fall under the AI Act. This becomes relevant in Chapter 9.

The ELIZA Effect

In 1966, Joseph Weizenbaum wrote ELIZA—a simple chatbot that simulated psychotherapist questions. Pure pattern matching. No intelligence. Yet people had emotional conversations with the program. Weizenbaum was perplexed.

In 1982, I wrote a similar program for my ZX81. 16 kilobytes of memory. Primitive rules. I knew exactly what was behind it—nothing. Yet the chats were strangely attractive.

This attraction persists today. People attribute understanding to a system that has none. With ELIZA, this was harmless. With an LLM analyzing drone specifications, it is dangerous.

The ELIZA effect leads to systematic overestimation. Those who have "conversations" with an AI underestimate how little is behind it. This is not a stupidity problem. This is a human problem. It affects engineers, CTOs, and decision-makers too.

Those who do not know this bias buy AI services with false expectations.

The Counterexample: Hyphenation

Not all problems could be solved with IF-THEN. German hyphenation is too complex for that. Too many exceptions, too many special cases. In our product M/TEXT (MANTEXT in the non-German World), the answer was not machine learning. The answer was gigantic word hyphenation tables. Complete enumeration instead of elegant rules.

That was expensive. That was laborious. But it was correct.

For critical applications, there were two options: Either you could guarantee correctness—or you did not do it. "Usually correct" was not an option for professional word processing.

With LLMs, complete enumeration is not possible. You cannot store all possible questions and all correct answers in advance. That is why "usually correct" with LLMs is not a bug but architecture.

The Spam Filter Paradox

Back to the spam filter. It pre-sorts emails. Practical. But legally?
Under Section 130 of the German Civil Code (BGB), an email is considered received when it is within the recipient's control. Whether you read it is irrelevant. You could have read it. If a notice of termination lands in the spam folder—legally, you were informed.

> Note for international readers: Similar principles apply in most jurisdictions under contract law—the concept of "constructive receipt" or "deemed delivery" when a message enters the recipient's control.

The spam filter shifts work but not responsibility. As a business owner, I still have to check my spam folder. That is why I do not use one.

The little helper does not really help. It just shifts the problem.

With an LLM for drone specifications, it is the same: The system can pre-sort, filter, summarize. But if it overlooks something important, the system is not liable. The engineer who should have checked is liable.

The TL;DR Paradox

"Too long; didn't read"—a standard comment on the internet. The answer? Have an LLM summarize it.

The LLM produces a summary. Helpful. But now there are more summaries, more "insights," more reports. More to read. So, you need more LLMs for more summaries.

A vicious cycle.

The irony: You may not be reading this book yourself. You may have an LLM summarize it. The LLM will tell you that LLMs have problems. You will nod and use it anyway.

That is not an accusation. That is human. But it explains why we need to have this conversation.

Machine Learning (1990s–2010s)

Instead of programming rules, you show the system examples. "This is spam. This is not spam. This is spam." After enough examples, the system recognizes patterns.

The human provides labeled data. The machine finds statistical correlations.

Strength: Learns from data. Finds patterns that humans overlook.

Weakness: Needs many labeled examples. Does not explain why it decides. The famous "black box."

Machine learning sorts your emails and recommends movies. It fails when the training data does not match reality.

Deep Learning (2010s–2020s)

Neural networks with many layers. Inspired by the brain, but only loosely. Like an airplane is inspired by a bird.

However, the comparison has two potential weak points. We do not entirely understand how artificial neural networks make their decisions. But we also do not really understand how biological neurons think. Clinical neurology has not mapped the connections of neural networks in the human brain. We are comparing something not understood with something else not understood—and calling it "explanation."

The numbers are staggering

The human brain contains about 86 billion neurons with roughly 100 trillion synapses. In the cerebral cortex alone: 125 trillion synapses—as many as stars in 1,500 Milky Ways [Stanford 2010].

But the decisive number is another: The number of possible connection patterns exceeds the number of atoms in the observable universe. The universe has an estimated 10^{80} atoms. The possible brain configurations are far above that.

And each individual synapse is not a simple switch. It functions more like a microprocessor with about 1,000 molecular switches [Stanford 2010].

We try to simulate this system with networks that have a few billion parameters. GPT-4 has an estimated 1.7 trillion parameters. That sounds like a lot, but it is only one percent of the synapses of a single human.

Deep learning no longer needs handcrafted features. It figures out what to pay attention to on its own. Facial recognition, speech recognition, image classification—all deep learning.

Strength: Recognizes complex patterns in images, speech, signals.

Weakness: Needs enormous computing power. Explains itself even less than machine learning. The black box becomes a black hole.

Large Language Models (since 2020)

LLMs are deep learning for language. Trained on half the internet. Billions of parameters. A single task: predict the next word.
That sounds banal. The results are not.

An LLM has no knowledge database. It has statistical weights that determine which word is likely to come next. It "understands" nothing. It approximates language.

Strength: Natural language. Context. Can answer questions no one has ever asked, or would even think of asking.

Weakness: Produces plausible-sounding answers—even when they are wrong. No knowledge, only probabilities.

2.1.2 The Crucial Difference

For our topic, one question counts: What happens with the same input?

Approach	Same Input →
Rule-based	Same output. Always.
Machine Learning	Same output. Stable after training.
Deep Learning	Same output. Deterministic.
LLM	**Different outputs possible.**

LLMs are stochastic. They roll dice—with loaded dice, but they roll.

Ask an LLM the same thing twice. You get two different answers. Not because it is defective. but because it was built that way. Variance is a feature, not a bug.

This is why traditional managed service contracts do not work.

An SLA guarantees: "For request X, we deliver result Y." That works for servers. That works for databases. That does not work for systems that deliver different results for the same request.

How do you write a maintenance contract for a system whose output is not predictable?

This question runs through the entire book.

2.1.3 Further Reading

For those who want to go deeper:

German-language: - Ertel, Wolfgang: *Grundkurs Künstliche Intelligenz.* Springer, 6th ed. 2025. – All AI subfields, understandable, with new LLM chapter. [Ertel 2025]

English (the standard work): - Russell, Stuart; Norvig, Peter: *Artificial Intelligence: A Modern Approach.* 4th Ed. 2020. – Used at over 1,500 universities. Comprehensive but demanding. [Russell/Norvig 2020]

Free online: - Google Developers: *Machine Learning Crash Course.* – Practice-oriented, with exercises. https://developers.google.com/machine-learning

2.2 The Promise for Drone Development

A drone swarm is not a toy.

In September 2025, a single computer controlled 15,947 drones simultaneously. World record. An entertainment show in China. 16,000 flying objects, choreographed to the centimeter.

Behind this is documentation. Mountains of it.

The Document Problem

A drone swarm project generates specifications for:

- RTK-GPS positioning (accuracy: 2 cm)
- Communication protocols (TDMA, bandwidth calculation)
- Collision avoidance (path calculation for 16,000 units)
- Energy management (flight time vs. payload)
- Security architecture (encryption, authentication)
- Emergency procedures (What happens on signal loss?)

Each of these areas has dependencies on the others. Path calculation affects energy consumption. Energy consumption determines flight time. Flight time limits choreography. Choreography defines communication load.

A typical project of this magnitude: 2,000 pages of specification. At minimum.

An engineer developing collision avoidance needs to know what the communications department wrote about latency times. Is the assumption of 15 ms per hop still valid? Or did someone correct that to 75 ms in a document the engineer never saw?

That is the daily reality. Not the exception.

The Promise

This is where AI comes in. The sales pitch sounds like this:

"Upload your 2,000 pages. Ask the system: Which assumptions about latency are contradictory? The AI finds it in seconds."

Specifically, the provider promises:

Task	Without AI	With AI
Finding contradictions	Days	Seconds
Searching specification	Hours	Seconds
Matching test protocol with requirements	Manual	Automatic
Onboarding new employees	Weeks	"Ask the AI"

That sounds like the solution to document chaos.

The Concrete Use Case

Imagine: An engineer works on collision avoidance. He asks the LLM: "Show me all places where latency assumptions for multi-hop communication are documented."

The system answers:

"In Document A (page 47) it says: 'Latency per hop: 10–20 ms typical.' In Document B (page 112) it says: 'Maximum latency with 5 hops: 325 ms.' In Document C (Test Protocol 23) it says: 'Measured latency: 47 ms average.' Possible contradiction: Document A implies 50–100 ms for 5 hops, Document B names 325 ms as maximum."

The engineer nods. Helpful. He would have needed hours to find that manually.

But did the LLM find all relevant passages? Or only those containing certain keywords? What about the section in Document D that uses "delay" instead of "latency"?

The engineer does not know. The LLM does not know. The provider does not know either.

Why It Is Tempting

The temptation is real. Drone development is complex. Documentation grows faster than the ability to read it. Every engineer knows the feeling: The answer is somewhere. But where?

A system that promises to "just ask" is attractive, especially for managers who do not know the technical details, but who do know the costs of documentation errors.

A crash due to inconsistent specifications does not just cost money. With drones over populated areas, it potentially costs lives.

The promise is: We eliminate this risk.

The problem: No one can keep this promise. The reason for this is explained in Chapter 5.

The Pattern

Drone development is just one example. The pattern repeats everywhere:

- Medical documentation (patient records, studies, guidelines)
- Legal research (contracts, rulings, commentaries)
- Regulatory compliance (standards, laws, audits)
- Software development (requirements, code, tests)

The same problem can be seen in many circumstances: Too much information. Too little overview. Too high costs for errors.

Everywhere the same promise: AI will solve it.

And everywhere the same question: Who checks if the AI is right?

2.3 Why In-House Development Seems Unaffordable

The promise from the last section sounds tempting. But why do companies buy AI as a service at all? Why don't they build it themselves?

The answer is simple: The cost.

The Four Cost Blocks

Anyone who wants to operate an LLM system for critical applications themselves faces four cost blocks. None of them is optional.

Cost Block 1: Expertise

An LLM does not operate itself. You need people who understand what they are doing.

Role	Task	Salary (Ger., 2025)
ML Engineer	Model selection, fine-tuning, optimization	€70,000–110,000
Data Scientist	Data preparation, evaluation, metrics	€65,000–100,000
MLOps Engineer	Deployment, monitoring, pipeline	€75,000–115,000
Prompt Engineer	Prompt design, quality assurance	€55,000–85,000

Minimum staffing for a productive system: 3–4 people. That is €250,000–400,000 in personnel costs per year. Just for operations.

The problem: These people are hard to find. There is no slack left in the market. Whoever finds them pays market prices. Whoever wants to keep them pays more.

Cost Block 2: Infrastructure

LLMs need computing power. A lot of it.

GPU Server (On-Premise): - NVIDIA H100 (80 GB): approx. €30,000 per card - A productive setup: 4–8 cards - Hardware investment: €120,000–240,000 - Lifespan: 3–4 years (then obsolete)

Ancillary costs: - Power: 3–5 kW per GPU, around the clock - Cooling: Data center class required - Network: 100 Gbit/s interconnect between GPUs

Cloud alternative: - AWS p5.48xlarge (8× H100): approx. $98/hour - 24/7 operation: approx. $860,000/year - Plus storage, network, backup

The cloud is not cheaper. It just shifts costs from Capex to Opex.

For detailed investment and operating costs of GPU infrastructure—including TCO calculations over five years and break-even analyses—see Appendix F.

Cost Block 3: Operations

A system that runs is not complete. It must be operated.

Monitoring: - Monitor model quality (drift detection) - Measure latency and throughput - Track costs per request - Detect anomalies

Updates: - Evaluate new model versions - Conduct regression tests - Maintain rollback strategies - Update documentation

Incident Response: - What happens when the model produces nonsense? - Who decides when to shut down? - How fast is the rollback?

Estimated costs: €100,000–150,000 per year. In addition to personnel costs.

Cost Block 4: Compliance

Since August 2024, the EU AI Act applies. Drone development falls under "high-risk" [AI Act 2024, Annex III]. This means:

Obligations: - Risk management system (Art. 9) - Data governance (Art. 10) - Technical documentation (Art. 11) - Record-keeping obligations (Art. 12) - Transparency (Art. 13) - Human oversight (Art. 14) - Accuracy, robustness, cybersecurity (Art. 15)

Costs: - Initial compliance review: €50,000–100,000 - Annual audits: €20,000–50,000 - Documentation and processes: €30,000–50,000 per year - Optional: ISO 42001 certification: €30,000–80,000

These are not "nice-to-have" expenses. These are legal obligations. Those who ignore them risk fines up to 35 million euros or 7% of global annual turnover [AI Act 2024, Art. 99].

The Total Bill

Cost Block	Year 1	Following Years
Expertise (Personnel)	€300,000	€300,000
Infrastructure (Hardware/Cloud)	€150,000	€100,000
Operations (Monitoring, Updates)	€100,000	€100,000
Compliance (Audits, Processes)	€100,000	€50,000
Total	**€650,000**	**€550,000**

These numbers are conservative. They apply to a medium-sized company with a single LLM use case. Those who operate multiple applications or have higher requirements multiply.

For a company with 50 million euros in revenue, 650,000 euros in the first year is 1.3% of revenue. Just for AI. Without a single value being realized.

Why It "Seems Unaffordable"

The costs are not the real problem. The real problem is uncertainty.
A company that invests 650,000 euros wants to know: What do I get for it?

With traditional software, the answer is clear: An ERP system books invoices. CAD software draws plans. The function is defined.

With an LLM, the answer is: It depends.

- How good is the training data?
- How precise are the prompts?
- How often does the model hallucinate?
- How much rework is needed?

No one can answer these questions beforehand. Not the provider. Not the consultant. Not even the ML engineer.

The 650,000 euros are a bet without guaranteed return.

The Analysts' View

Forrester predicts for 2026: Ungoverned generative AI will cost B2B companies more than 10 billion US dollars [Forrester 2025] in falling stock prices, legal settlements, and regulatory penalties.

The recommendation: Enable employees to "identify bad results before they are implemented."

That sounds reasonable. But it also means: The human remains responsible. AI delivers suggestions. The human checks and bears the consequences.

Forrester calls this the "renaissance of human expertise." GenAI delivers "more information—or misinformation." Buyers turn to experts "to validate insights" [Forrester 2025].

The analysts are saying it themselves: AI does not replace the expert. It creates validation needs.

But validation costs a lot. Personnel. Time. Competence. Exactly the resources one wanted to save through AI.

The Dilemma

The situation is paradoxical:

1. **In-house development is expensive.** €650,000 in the first year, €550,000 in following years. Plus risk, plus uncertainty.
2. **In-house development is necessary.** Those who want to validate need competence. Those who have competence can also operate themselves.
3. **Without in-house capability: dependency.** Those who cannot evaluate results buy blind.

This is why managed service seems so attractive. Someone else bears the costs. Someone else is expected to be competent. Someone else takes the responsibility.

Whether that works is examined in the next section.

2.4 The Managed Service Temptation

€650,000 in the first year. €550,000 in following years. Plus risk. Plus uncertainty.

Then comes the offer: €12,000 per month. Everything included.

The Promise

The managed service provider promises:

In-House	Managed Service
Hire 4 specialists	Expertise included
Buy GPU servers	Infrastructure included
Build monitoring	Operations included
Ensure compliance	"We take care of it"
€650,000/year	**€144,000/year**

The calculation is simple: Factor 4.5. For a quarter of the cost, you get everything you need.

That sounds like a good deal.

The Logic Behind It

Managed services work through economies of scale. A provider serving 100 customers can share costs:

Personnel: - One ML engineer serves not one customer but twenty. - Cost per customer: not €100,000 but €5,000.

Infrastructure: - GPU clusters are shared. - Utilization rises from 30% to 80%. - Cost per request decreases.

Know-how: - Problems solved once stay solved. - Best practices are reused. – The learning curve is distributed across all customers.

This is the classic managed service model. It works for data centers. It works for SAP operations. It works for security operations.

Why should it not work for AI?

The Comparison with Traditional IT

With a traditional managed service—let's say: server operations—the model looks like this:

1. **Standardization:** Servers are servers. Windows is Windows. The problems are known.
2. **Transparency:** The service provider sees everything. Logs, metrics, configurations. He can diagnose.
3. **Predictability:** A server that runs today runs tomorrow too. Failures have causes. Causes can be fixed.

4. **Measurability:** Availability is measurable. 99.9% means 8.7 hours of downtime per year. No more, no less.

This allows an SLA. The service provider guarantees availability. The customer pays. Both know where they stand.

The Pricing

Typical offers for "AI as a Service" in the B2B space:

Service Level	Monthly Price
Basic (API access, standard model)	€2,000–5,000
Professional (Fine-tuning, support)	€5,000–15,000
Enterprise (dedicated instance, SLA)	€15,000–50,000

Even the Enterprise package costs €600,000 per year—less than in-house, and you have a contact person when something does not work.

At least in theory.

Why It Seems Logical

The decision for managed service is not stupidity. It is economically rational—under certain assumptions:

Assumption 1: The service provider has the expertise. → Probably. Large providers have ML teams.

Assumption 2: The infrastructure can be shared. → Partially. Inference can be shared. Training is harder.

Assumption 3: The service provider can guarantee quality. → This is where it gets problematic.

Assumption 4: The service provider assumes responsibility. → This is where the model collapses.

The Unspoken Expectation

Those who buy a managed service expect more than infrastructure. They expect results.

With server hosting, the result is clear: The server runs or it does not.

With an LLM service, the result is unclear: The answer is correct. Or it sounds correct but is wrong.

The customer expects: "You take care of making the AI work."

The provider means: "We ensure that the AI responds."

That is not the same thing.

The Temptation

The temptation of managed service is not the price alone. It is the promise of getting rid of a problem.

AI is complex. AI is new. AI is risky.

The managed service promises: You do not have to understand this. We understand it for you.

That is attractive. Especially for decision-makers who are not AI experts. Especially in companies that want to act quickly. Especially when the competition is already "using AI."

The question is: Can this promise be kept?

The answer comes in the next section.

2.5 Why It Does Not Work This Time

The managed service model works. For servers. For networks. For SAP systems.

For LLMs, it does not work.

The reason is structural.

What Works with Traditional IT

A Managed Service Provider (MSP) for server operations works like this:

Complete visibility: - The MSP sees all logs. - The MSP sees all metrics. - The MSP sees all configurations. - The MSP sees all error messages.

Standardized environment: - Windows Server is Windows Server. - VMware is VMware. - The problems are documented. - The solutions are known.

Replicable errors: - An error has a cause. - The cause can be found. - The solution can be tested. - The error no longer occurs.

This allows division of labor. The MSP knows the technology. The customer knows his business. Both do not have to know everything.

What Is Different with LLMs

With an LLM for critical applications—such as drone development—the situation looks different.

Problem 1: The MSP Is Not Allowed to See

The 2,000 pages of drone specifications are confidential. They contain:

- Technical details (communication protocols, encryption)
- Trade secrets (algorithms, optimizations)
- Possibly: Dual-use relevant information

The customer cannot give these documents to an external service provider. Not from mistrust. For legal reasons.

But these documents are exactly the basis for the LLM. The fine-tuning. The RAG system. The prompts.

> The MSP is supposed to maintain a system whose content he is not allowed to know.

Problem 2: Every Customer Is Different

With server operations, the MSP can transfer experience. A Windows problem at Customer A is also a Windows problem at Customer B.

With LLMs, this does not apply.

- Customer A has drone specifications.
- Customer B has patient records.
- Customer C has contract documents.

The data structures are different. The technical language is different. The quality criteria are different.

What works at Customer A says nothing about Customer B.

> Economies of scale through knowledge transfer do not work.

Problem 3: Errors Are Not Replicable

With a server, an error is an event. It happens, it is logged, it is analyzed, it is fixed.

With an LLM, an "error" is a wrong answer.

- Why was the answer wrong?
- Was it the model? The prompt? The training data?
- Would the same question produce the same wrong answer?
- Probably not. The system is stochastic.

> Error analysis in the traditional sense: not possible.

Problem 4: Quality Is Not Measurable

The MSP can measure: - Response time: 1.2 seconds. ✓ - Availability: 99.9%. ✓ - Throughput: 1,000 requests per minute. ✓

The MSP cannot measure: - Was the answer correct? - Was the answer complete? - Did the LLM overlook something important?

For that, the MSP would have to understand the content. The drone specification. The technical terms. The connections.

Only the customer can do that. Or someone with the same expertise.

The Paradox

The situation is paradoxical:

To maintain, one must see. → The MSP would have to know the data to assess quality.

To see, one needs access. → The customer would have to release the data.

Access is forbidden. → Confidentiality, trade secrets, compliance.

So the MSP cannot maintain. → He can only provide infrastructure.

What the MSP Actually Delivers

If you look closely, an "AI Managed Service" for critical applications delivers:

Promised	Delivered
"We operate your AI"	We operate the infrastructure
"Experts take care of it"	Experts for ML-Ops, not for your domain
"Quality guarantee"	Availability guarantee
"Everything from one source"	Technology from one source, validation remains your responsibility

This is not fraud. This is a misunderstanding. The customer expects more than the model can deliver.

The Comparison

Aspect	Server Operations	LLM Operations
Data visible to MSP	Yes (logs, metrics)	No (confidential)
Problems standardized	Yes (known errors)	No (context-dependent)
Errors replicable	Yes (deterministic)	No (stochastic)
Quality measurable	Yes (availability)	No (correctness)
Knowledge transfer possible	Yes (same technology)	No (different data)
Economies of Scale	**Work**	**Do Not Work**

The Consequence

The managed service model is based on economies of scale. A provider shares costs across many customers.

With LLMs for critical applications, these economies of scale do not exist:

- Every customer has different data.
- Every customer has different quality criteria.
- Every customer needs different domain expertise for validation.

The provider can share infrastructure. He can share ML-Ops. He can share support processes.

He cannot share what constitutes the actual value: The ability to judge whether the answer is correct.

> This ability remains with the customer. Always.

2.6 The Economic Paradox

Let us summarize.

The Starting Point

A company wants to use AI for critical applications. Drone development. Medical documentation. Legal research. Some area where errors have impactful consequences.

Option 1: In-House Development

- €650,000 in the first year
- €550,000 in following years
- Plus: Competence stays in-house
- Plus: Full control
- Minus: Risk whether it works
- Minus: Too expensive for most companies

Option 2: Managed Service

- €144,000 per year
- Minus: Economies of scale do not work
- Minus: Quality cannot be guaranteed
- Minus: Responsibility stays with the customer anyway
- Result: You pay for infrastructure, not for results

The Paradox

The paradox has two sides:

Side 1: In-house development is unaffordable

For a company with 50 million euros in revenue, €650,000 per year is 1.3% of revenue. Just for AI operations. Without guaranteed benefit.

This only pays off if the benefit exceeds the costs. With experimental technologies, this benefit is not anticipatable.

> Most companies cannot afford in-house development.

Side 2: Managed service does not solve the problem

The managed service costs less. But it also delivers less:

- Infrastructure: yes
- Availability: yes
- Correctness: no
- Validation: no
- Responsibility: no

The customer saves on costs. He does not save on competence. He needs that anyway—to check if the AI is right.

> Those without competence buy blind. Those with competence need the service less.

The Calculation That Does Not Add Up

Cost Type	In-House	Managed Service
Infrastructure	€150,000	included
ML-Ops	€100,000	included
Compliance infrastructure	€50,000	partially included
Domain expertise for validation	**€300,000**	**€300,000**
Total Costs	**€600,000**	**€444,000**

The savings shrink. From factor 4.5 to factor 1.4.

And that only if one assumes that the managed service completely takes over the technical tasks. For critical applications, this is doubtful.

The Hidden Costs of Managed Service

What the price comparison does not show:

Coordination overhead: - Coordination with the service provider - Explaining requirements - Review of results - Escalations for problems

Loss of control: - Dependency on response times - No direct insight into problems - Vendor lock-in

Compliance risk: - The AI Act makes the deployer responsible - "We have a service provider" is no relief - The regulator does not ask the MSP, they ask you

The Three Scenarios

For companies that want to use AI for critical applications, there are three scenarios:

Scenario A: In-house with full competence - Investment: €600,000–800,000 per year - Prerequisites: Budget, talent, strategic priority - Result: Full control, full responsibility, full risk - Suitable for: Large enterprises, tech companies, strategic applications

Scenario B: Managed service with internal validation - Investment: €150,000 service + €300,000 internal validation = €450,000 - Prerequisites: Subject matter experts who can evaluate AI results - Result: Shared costs, shared responsibility (but legally with the customer) - Suitable for: Mid-sized companies with domain competence

Scenario C: Managed service without validation competence - Investment: €150,000 service - Prerequisites: Trust in the provider - Result: Cheap but blind - Suitable for: Non-critical applications. Not for drones. Not for medicine. Not for law.

The Uncomfortable Truth

There is no cheap solution for AI in critical applications.

- In-house development is expensive.
- Managed service does not help you save the capital you had hoped.
- Validation competence is always needed.

This is not market failure. This is the structure of the technology.

A stochastic system whose outputs are not predictable cannot be maintained like a deterministic system. The service provider can keep the machine running. He cannot guarantee that the machine is right.

> No one can give that guarantee.

2.7 Key Points

- **LLMs are stochastic.** Same input, different outputs. This is not a bug, this is the architecture.
- **The promise is attractive.** Search 2,000 pages in seconds. Find contradictions. Master document chaos.

- **In-house development costs €500,000–800,000 per year.** Personnel, infrastructure, operations, compliance.
- **Managed service saves less than hoped.** Validation responsibility stays with the customer.
- **Economies of scale do not work.** Every customer has different data, different quality criteria, different validation needs.
- **There is no cheap solution.** Those who want AI for critical applications need competence. Competence costs.

Chapter 2 analyzed the promise and revealed the cost structure. Chapter 3 examines what local LLMs change—and what they do not.

Chapter 3: What Local LLMs Can Do—And What They Cannot

An objection suggests itself: "If the managed service does not work—why don't we just run the LLM locally?"

The idea is attractive. No cloud. No data transfer. Full control.
But does that solve the problems from Chapter 2?

3.1 Technical Foundations: Inference, Fine-Tuning, RAG

Before we answer the question "If the managed service does not work—why don't we just run the LLM locally?", we need to clarify what "running locally" actually means. There are three approaches—and they solve different problems.

Inference: Running the Model Locally

The simplest scenario: You take a pre-trained model (such as Llama, Mistral, or another open-source LLM) and run it on your own hardware.

What this solves: - Data does not leave the company - No dependency on API availability - No ongoing API costs - Full control over model version

What this does not solve: - The model does not know your domain - The model produces the same wrong answers as in the cloud - Quality depends on the base model

Hardware requirements: - 7B model (e.g., Llama 3.1 7B): 8–16 GB VRAM, runs on consumer GPU - 70B model (e.g., Llama 3.1 70B): 40–80 GB VRAM, requires professional hardware - 405B model: Multiple high-end GPUs, data center class

For critical applications, smaller models are often insufficient. The larger ones require significant investments—see Chapter 2.3 and Appendix F for detailed TCO calculations.

Fine-Tuning: Adapting the Model

Fine-tuning means: You continue training an existing model on your own data. The model "learns" the technical language, the document structure, the specific relationships.

What this solves: - Better adaptation to the domain - Model knows technical terms and jargon - Potentially higher quality for specific tasks

What this does not solve: - Wrong answers do not disappear - The model can incorrectly combine what it learned - Training requires ML expertise and computing power - Every update to base data requires new training

The fundamental problem:

Fine-tuning changes the model's weights. It makes the model "more familiar" with your domain. But it does not make the model "more reliable" in the sense of deterministic.

A fine-tuned model still produces stochastic outputs. It still delivers plausible lies—only now with your technical terminology.

RAG: Retrieval-Augmented Generation

RAG is currently the most popular approach. The idea: The model receives relevant documents with each query. It generates answers based on these documents.

The process: 1. User asks question 2. System searches for relevant documents (Retrieval) 3. Documents are passed to the model as context 4. Model generates answer based on context

What this solves: - Model does not have to "know" everything—it gets sources - Updated documents are immediately available (no retraining) - Answers can include source citations - Data protection: Documents stay local

What this does not solve:

Problem 1: Retrieval Quality

The retrieval step does not always find the right documents. A document that uses "delay" instead of "latency" may not be found.

This is not a theoretical problem. In the 2,000 pages of drone specification, there are different authors, different terminology, different document structures.

The Compound Word Problem: German Is Poison for Retrieval

The German language has a characteristic that poses special problems for retrieval systems: word composition.

In English, you write: "communication protocol specification". Three words. Each individually searchable.

In German, you write: "Kommunikationsprotokollspezifikation". One word. 36 letters.

The classic example is the "Donaudampfschifffahrtskapitänskajütenschranktürenschlossschraube" (Danube steamship captain's cabin wardrobe door lock screw). 51 letters, one word. Theoretically correct German. Practically a nightmare for any search system.

For drone development, this is relevant:

Document contains	Engineer asks	Retrieval finds
"Flugbahnberechnungsalgorithmus" (trajectory calculation algorithm)	"How is the trajectory calculated?"	Probably nothing
"Signallaufzeitmessung" (signal propagation time measurement)	"Measure latency"	Probably nothing
"Störsignalunterdrückungsverfahren" (interference signal suppression method)	"How do you filter noise?"	Probably nothing

The embedding models used for retrieval were predominantly trained on English texts. They break words into tokens. This works better with "communication protocol" than with "Kommunikationsprotokoll".

The result: The engineer asks about the screw for the lock of the door of the wardrobe of the cabin of the captain of the steamship on the Danube. The system does not find the document—because it searches for individual terms that do not appear in this form.

This is not a fringe problem. German technical documentation is full of compound words. Anyone deploying RAG on German technical texts must solve this problem—or accept that relevant documents will be overlooked.

> Note for international readers: While German compound words are an extreme example, similar challenges exist in other languages with agglutinative features (Finnish, Turkish) or when technical documents use inconsistent terminology across authors and departments.

Problem 2: Context Window

Even modern LLMs have limited context windows. 128,000 tokens sounds like a lot—but 2,000 pages is more.

The system must choose which documents to show the model. This selection can be wrong.

Problem 3: Plausible Lies Despite Context

Even with correct documents in context, the model can produce wrong answers. It can: - Incorrectly combine information from different documents - "Add" details that are not in the sources - Invent source citations

Studies show: RAG reduces the frequency of wrong answers but does not eliminate them.

3.2 Wrong Answers Are Not a Cloud Problem

A widespread misunderstanding: "In the cloud, the model delivers wrong answers because it was trained on foreign data. Locally, we have control."

This is false.

The Cause of Wrong Answers

Important: The industry speaks of "hallucination." This term is misleading. A hallucination is a perceptual disorder—something that should not be. With LLMs, there is no disorder. The system works exactly as designed.

An LLM is a statistical model. It was trained to generate plausible continuations. "Plausible" means: statistically probable, given the context.

"Plausible" does not mean factually correct.

The model has no concept of "true" or "false." It has probability distributions. When the most probable continuation is wrong, the model produces a wrong answer—with full confidence.

This is not a bug. This is the architecture.

Cloud vs. Local: No Difference

Property	Cloud LLM	Local LLM
Architecture	Transformer	Transformer
Training method	Next-token prediction	Next-token prediction
Output	Stochastic	Stochastic
Wrong answers	Yes, system-inherent	Yes, system-inherent

The model does not know where it runs. It does not know whose data it processes. It generates outputs according to the same principles—whether on an AWS server or in your own data center.

What Local Actually Solves

Local operation solves real problems–but different ones:

Data protection: Queries and documents do not leave the company. No transfer to third parties. No cloud logging by the provider.

Availability: No dependency on internet connectivity or API outages.

Version control: You can freeze and test a specific model version. No "We improved the model" overnight.

Cost predictability: Fixed costs instead of usage-based billing.

These are real advantages. But none of them concerns the quality of outputs.

3.3 Local Control ≠ Quality Control

The term "control" is used in two meanings. This leads to confusion.

Control Type 1: Infrastructure Control

- We determine which hardware is used
- We determine which model version runs
- We determine who has access
- We determine where data is stored

This control is real and valuable.

Control Type 2: Quality Control

- We determine that the model gives correct answers
- We guarantee that no wrong answers occur
- We ensure that nothing is overlooked

This control is an illusion.

The Difference

Infrastructure control is like owning a printing press. You determine what gets printed. You determine who has access. You determine which paper is used.

But you do not control whether what is printed is true.

A local LLM is like owning your own printing press for texts. You have full control over the machine. You have no control over the quality of what it produces.

The Practical Consequence

A company that operates an LLM locally must still:

1. **Verify every output**–the model can be wrong

2. **Deploy domain experts**—verification requires domain knowledge
3. **Establish processes**—who verifies, who approves, who is liable
4. **Document**—for audits, compliance, traceability

None of this becomes unnecessary through local operation.

The Trap of False Security

Local operation can even be more dangerous than cloud usage.

Why?

With cloud services, distrust is built in. Everyone knows: "This is an external service, I have to be careful."

With local systems, a false sense of security arises: "This is our system, on our servers, with our data. We can trust this."

No. The system does not deserve more trust just because it runs locally. The architecture is the same. The error sources are the same. Validation is just as necessary.

3.4 Key Points

- **Local operation solves the data protection problem.** Documents stay in the company. No data transfer to third parties.
- **Local operation does not solve the quality problem.** Wrong answers are architecture-inherent, not location-inherent.
- **Fine-tuning makes the model more familiar, not more reliable.** It knows your terminology. It still makes mistakes.
- **RAG reduces wrong answers, does not eliminate them.** Retrieval errors and context limits remain. German compound words exacerbate the problem.
- **Infrastructure control is not quality control.** Owning the machine does not control what it produces.
- **The validation requirement remains.** Whether cloud or local—someone must verify whether the answer is correct.

Local LLMs shift the problem, they do not solve it. The question remains: Who validates? This leads to the core metaphor of this book. Chapter 4 explains the Little Helper Paradox.

Chapter 4: The Little Helper Paradox

In the Disney comics, Gyro Gearloose has an assistant. A small creature with a light bulb on its head. It is called the Little Helper.

Figure 3 The more the system helps, the less is verified. The less is verified, the more dangerous the undetected risk becomes – a self-reinforcing cycle.

The Little Helper is useful. It hands over tools. It holds things in place. It makes the laboratory a little less chaotic.

But the Little Helper is not an engineer. It does not understand what Gyro Gearloose is building. It has no idea about physics, mechanics, or the art of invention. It helps—without understanding what it is helping with.

This is the perfect metaphor for LLMs in critical applications.

4.1 Gyro Gearloose's Assistant as Metaphor

Imagine: Gyro Gearloose is building a flying machine. Complicated construction. Hundreds of parts.

He says to the Little Helper: "Hand me the screw for the elevator."

The Little Helper knows screws. It even knows the word "elevator." But it does not understand why this specific screw is important. It does not understand that a wrong screw can lead to a crash.

So, it hands over a screw. Any screw. It looks similar. Fits approximately.

Gyro Gearloose—the expert—must check. Is it the right screw? The right diameter? The right material? The right strength class?

If he does not check, the machine flies. Maybe. Or it crashes.

The Little Helper helped. But the responsibility? That lies with the inventor.

4.2 Assistance Without Understanding

An LLM is a Little Helper for knowledge work.

It can:

- Summarize texts
- Search documents
- Suggest formulations
- Recognize patterns
- Answer questions

It cannot:

- Understand what it is doing
- Know whether the answer is correct
- Assess the consequences of a wrong answer
- Take responsibility

The LLM hands over screws. Quickly. Efficiently. In large quantities.

But it does not know which screw is the right one. It does not even know that it does not know. It hands over what is statistically most likely to fit.

> This is not a deficiency. This is the architecture.

An LLM was trained to generate plausible answers. Not correct ones. Not responsible ones. Plausible ones.

Plausible and correct are often the same thing. But not always. And for critical applications, "often" is not good enough.

4.3 The Illusion of Control

The Little Helper Paradox has a treacherous property: It creates the illusion of control.

The illusion:

- The system answers questions → It understands the questions

- The system cites sources → It has read the sources
- The system formulates precisely → It knows what it is talking about
- The system says "I am not sure" → It can assess uncertainty

The reality:

- The system generates probable word combinations
- The source citations can be invented
- Precise formulation says nothing about correctness
- "I am not sure" is a trained phrase, not genuine self-assessment

The Little Helper appears competent. It speaks in complete sentences. It does not contradict. It always delivers an answer.

This makes it more dangerous than an obviously dumb tool.

A calculator shows "Error" when you divide by zero. An LLM invents a plausible answer.

4.4 The Paradox

The actual paradox lies in the structure of helping:

Thesis: The LLM is supposed to take work off your hands.

Antithesis: Every output must be verified.

Synthesis: The verification is often more laborious than the original work.

Concretely:

An engineer asks: "Which latency assumptions contradict each other?"

The LLM delivers a list. Five alleged contradictions. With page numbers. With quotes.

Now the engineer must:

1. Verify each source citation—is the page number correct?
2. Verify each quote—does it really say that there?
3. Analyze each alleged contradiction—is it really a contradiction?
4. Check what is missing—did the LLM overlook something?

Point 4 is the hardest. To know what is missing, the engineer must search himself. With different search terms. With different context.

In the end, the engineer has done the work by himself anyway, plus the work of checking the LLM output.

> The Little Helper did not help. It created additional work.

4.5 When the Little Helper Actually Helps

The paradox is not total. There are use cases where the Little Helper actually helps:

When errors are tolerable:

- Brainstorming, idea generation
- First drafts that will be revised
- Summaries for overview, not for decisions

When verification is easy:

- Code that compiles or does not (syntax errors visible)
- Translations that a native speaker quickly checks
- Formatting that can be visually verified

When the human remains involved anyway:

- The LLM as research assistant, not as decision-maker
- Suggestions that are discussed
- Drafts that an expert revises
- The pattern is clear: The Little Helper helps when a human retains control and verification is feasible.

For critical applications—drone specifications, medical documentation, legal research—verification is not feasible. Not for every query. Not with the required diligence.

4.6 The Consequence for Managed Services

Now it becomes clear why "AI as Managed Service" does not work for critical applications:

The MSP can operate the Little Helper.

- Provide servers: yes
- Deploy model: yes
- Guarantee availability: yes

The MSP cannot validate the Little Helper.

- Check whether the answer is correct: no
- Know what is missing: no
- Provide domain assessment: no

Validation requires domain expertise. The customer has that. Or no one does.

If the customer has the expertise, he can also check himself whether the Little Helper is right. Then he only needs the MSP for infrastructure.

If the customer does not have the expertise, no one can check. Then the system is unusable—regardless of who operates it.

This is the Little Helper Paradox in its economic form:

- Those who can validate need the service less
- Those who cannot validate cannot use the service
- There is no customer group for whom the model works

4.7 Key Points

- **The LLM is a Little Helper.** It assists without understanding. It hands over screws without knowing which one fits.
- **The competence illusion is dangerous.** The system appears competent. It is not competent. It is statistically plausible.
- **Verification creates additional work.** Those who must validate every output do not save time. They invest time in checking.
- **Tolerable errors are the key.** The Little Helper helps where errors are correctable. It fails where errors have consequences.
- **The validation gap cannot be closed.** Those who lack the domain expertise to verify cannot safely use the system.
- **The economic paradox:** For critical applications, there is no customer group for whom "AI as Managed Service" works.

The Little Helper Paradox explains why responsibility remains with the human. Part 2 of the book will show how this paradox manifests in concrete contract attempts. Chapter 5 begins with the SLA test: What happens when you try to write a maintenance contract?

Part 2: The Falsification

Chapter 5: The SLA Test—Availability vs. Correctness

Part 1 analyzed the promise. Part 2 tests it.

The method is simple: We try to write a contract. A real managed service contract for an LLM system in critical applications.

If it is possible, writing should succeed. If it is not possible, the attempt will fail—and the failure shows why.

5.1 The SLA Falsification Method: Try to Write the Contract

A Service Level Agreement (SLA) defines what the service provider delivers and what happens if he does not deliver it.

For traditional IT services, it looks like this:

Example: Server Hosting

Parameter	Commitment	Measurement	Consequence for Violation
Availability	99.9%	Monitoring (Uptime)	Credit 10% of monthly fee
Response time	< 100 ms	Latency measurement	Credit 5%
Data backup	Daily	Backup protocol	Contractual penalty

This works because: 1. The parameters are measurable 2. The measurement is objective 3. The consequences are calculable

Now we try the same for an LLM system.

5.2 Availability: Measurable

Let us start with the simple part.

SLA Draft: Availability

Parameter	Commitment	Measurement
System availability	99.5%	Uptime monitoring
API reachability	99.9%	Health checks
Maximum downtime	4 hours continuous	Incident tickets

This can be written. This can be measured. This can be guaranteed.

A provider can commit: "The system responds." He can back this commitment with technology: redundancy, failover, monitoring.

Assessment: ✓ Possible Criminal Law Tractability: An Underestimated Quality Feature

With traditional IT, there is an aspect that is rarely discussed: When something goes wrong, you can investigate.

Traditional IT incidents and their tractability:

Incident	Criminal Code	Investigation Possible
Unauthorized data access	Computer fraud / unauthorized access statutes	Yes—logs, timestamps, IP addresses
Data manipulation	Data tampering laws	Yes—audit trail, versioning
System sabotage	Computer sabotage statutes	Yes—forensics, network analysis
Falsified logs	Forgery of evidentiary data	Yes—hash comparison, metadata
Fraud through IT manipulation	Computer fraud	Yes—transaction logs

Note for international readers: While specific statute numbers vary by jurisdiction (German StGB §§ 202a, 303a, 303b, 269, 263a referenced in the original), virtually all developed legal systems have equivalent criminal provisions for computer crimes. The key point is that traditional IT incidents leave forensic traces that enable criminal prosecution.

Criminal procedure law provides tools: seizure of servers, analysis of logs, expert opinions. There is a perpetrator, a means, a time, causality.

With an LLM that gives a wrong answer:

Question	Problem
Who is the perpetrator?	The model? The prompt? The training data? The provider? The user?
What is the act?	Wrong output—but system-inherent, no intent
When did it happen?	At the query? During training? At the architecture decision?
How do you prove causality?	Stochastic system—same query yields different output
Criminal prosecution?	Against whom? For what?

The prosecutor has nothing to work with.

A server that deletes data has logs. An employee who manipulates leaves traces. An LLM that produces a plausible lie functions as designed.

There is no perpetrator in the criminal law sense. There is no means—the model is the product. There is no intent—the system "wants" nothing.

The Trust Paradox: Human vs. Machine

A personal example: This book contains legal explanations. The author is not a lawyer. He says so. The reader knows it. The book does not replace legal advice—it says so in the foreword.

When an LLM cites the same statutes: Who is the "author"? Where is the disclaimer? And why should one trust a system that does not know its limits—while distrusting a human who names his limits?

The human who says "I am not a lawyer" is more trustworthy than the system that sounds like a lawyer. The human knows his limits. The system knows no limits—because it does not know what it does not know.

This is not a plea for modesty. It is a pointer to an asymmetry: We require qualification proofs from humans. From LLMs we require nothing—and trust them anyway.

The consequence for contracts:

With traditional IT services, an SLA can refer to criminal consequences: "In case of intentional manipulation, we reserve the right to take legal action." This has a preventive effect.

With LLM services, this threat is empty. Wrong answers are not a crime. They are statistics.

5.3 Correctness: Not Guaranteed

Now it gets difficult.

SLA Draft: Correctness (Attempt 1)

Parameter	Commitment	Measurement
Correct answers	95%	???

How do you measure "correct"?

Problem 1: Who defines "correct"?

For the question "Which latency assumptions contradict each other?" there is no objective answer. There are: - Answers that the engineer considers correct - Answers that another engineer evaluates differently - Answers that are correct today and outdated tomorrow

Correctness is context-dependent, expert-dependent, and time-dependent.

Problem 2: Who measures?

The MSP cannot measure. He does not know the domain. He does not know whether "Latency 15 ms" is a correct statement.

The customer would have to measure. But if the customer checks every answer for correctness, he does not need the service.

Problem 3: When do you measure?

With a server, you know immediately whether it is running. With an LLM answer, you only know later whether it was correct—sometimes only when the drone has crashed.

SLA Draft: Correctness (Attempt 2)

Parameter	Commitment	Measurement
No demonstrably wrong answers	100%	Customer complaint

This shifts the problem. Now the customer must prove that the answer was wrong. After damage. In court.

This is not an SLA. This is a liability clause, and one that the provider will not sign.

SLA Draft: Correctness (Attempt 3)

Parameter	Commitment	Measurement
Answers based on provided documents	"Best Effort"	Not defined

"Best Effort" means: no guarantee. The provider tries. If it does not work, it is not his problem.

This is the formulation that actually appears in contracts.

Assessment: X Not Possible

There is no formulation that guarantees correctness and is simultaneously: - measurable - objectively verifiable - attributable to the provider

5.4 Response Time vs. Answer Quality

A popular escape route: You do not define correctness but response time.

SLA Draft: Response Time

Parameter	Commitment	Measurement
Response time (API)	< 2 seconds	Server logs
Response time (Support)	< 4 hours	Ticket system
Escalation for critical errors	< 1 hour	Incident management

This is measurable. This is guaranteed. This is sensible.

But it answers the wrong question.

The customer wants to know: Is the answer correct?

The SLA guarantees: The answer comes quickly.

A fast wrong answer is not better than a slow wrong answer. It is even more dangerous—because it creates the appearance of efficiency.

The Shift

Every SLA for LLM services shifts the guarantee from what matters to what is measurable:

What Matters	What Is Guaranteed
Correctness	Availability
Completeness	Response time
No errors	"Best Effort"
Domain suitability	Technical function

This is not malice. It is the only way to write a contract that is legally tenable.

The consequence: The contract guarantees that the system runs. It does not guarantee that it is useful.

Figure 4 An SLA for LLM correctness fails due to measurability. What you cannot measure, you cannot guarantee.

5.5 The Complete SLA Attempt

Let us summarize. A realistic SLA for "AI as a Service" looks like this:

Guaranteed:

Parameter	Commitment	Service Credit for Violation
Availability	99.5%	10% monthly fee
API latency	< 2 seconds	5% monthly fee
Support response	< 4 hours	None
Data backup	Daily	Contractual penalty
Data protection	GDPR-compliant	Contractual penalty

Not guaranteed (expressly excluded):

- Correctness of generated answers
- Completeness of research results
- Suitability for specific application purposes
- Freedom from errors or omissions

- Consistency with source documents

Standard clause:

> *"The provider assumes no warranty for the substantive correctness, completeness, or currency of outputs generated by the system. Use of the outputs is at the customer's own risk. The customer is obligated to independently verify all outputs before use."*

This is an honest SLA. It describes what the provider can deliver.

It also describes what "Managed Service" means for LLMs: **Managed Infrastructure. Not Managed Intelligence.**

5.6 The Falsification

The SLA method has delivered its result:

Claim: "We offer AI as Managed Service."

Test: Write an SLA that guarantees what matters.

Result: Impossible. What matters (correctness) cannot be guaranteed.

Conclusion: "AI as Managed Service" is a deceptive package. What is sold is infrastructure. What is implied is quality. What is delivered is infrastructure.

This is not a conspiracy. It is a structural problem. No provider can guarantee correctness–because correctness can not be guaranteed with stochastic systems.

And unlike with traditional IT problems, there is no criminal law fallback. No prosecutor can investigate when the system functions as designed and is still wrong.

5.7 Key Points

- **Availability cannot be guaranteed.** The system runs. This can be measured and committed to.
- **Correctness cannot be guaranteed.** No formulation manages to define correctness in a way that is measurable, objective, and attributable.
- **Traditional IT is forensically tractable.** With manipulation, there is a perpetrator, a means, traces. With LLM errors, there is none of that.
- **Humans with limits are more trustworthy than systems without limits.** Those who say "I am not a lawyer" deserve more trust than a system that sounds like a lawyer but is not one.

- **SLAs shift the guarantee.** What matters (correctness) is excluded. What is measurable (availability) is guaranteed.
- **"Best Effort" is not a guarantee.** It is the absence of a guarantee in polite language.
- **The standard clause says everything:** "Use at own risk. Verification by customer required."
- **Managed Service for LLMs = Managed Infrastructure.** Nothing more. Those who expect more will be disappointed.

The SLA test shows: Correctness cannot be contractually assured. But why is that? Chapter 6 explains why wrong answers are not a bug but a feature—the plausible lie as a system property.

Chapter 6: Plausible Lie as Feature

The industry has a word for wrong LLM answers: "hallucination."

The word is wrong. It obscures what actually happens. And it prevents us from understanding the problem correctly.

6.1 Why "Hallucination" Is the Wrong Term

A hallucination is a perceptual disorder. A person sees something that is not there. Hears voices that no one speaks. The brain produces sensory impressions without external stimulus.

The crucial point: A hallucination is pathological. It is a symptom. It shows that something is not functioning as intended.

With an LLM, the opposite is the case.

When an LLM produces a wrong answer: - The system functions exactly as built - The algorithm works flawlessly - The hardware has no problem - The software has no bug

The system does what it is supposed to do: It generates the most probable continuation. That this continuation is factually wrong is not due to a malfunction. It is due to the architecture.

The term "hallucination" is an anthropomorphization. It suggests the system has a "normal" function (correct answers) and sometimes a "disturbed" function (wrong answers). This is false.

The system has only one function: token prediction. Whether the result is correct is irrelevant to the system. It optimizes for plausibility, not for truth.

The Danger of the Wrong Metaphor

Those who say "hallucination" automatically think: - This is an exceptional state - This can be treated - This will improve when we "heal" the system

Those who understand that wrong answers are system-inherent think differently: - This is the normal state - This cannot be patched away - This remains as long as the architecture remains

The metaphor determines the expectation. The expectation determines the decision. Those who believe "hallucinations" are a solvable problem buy a service hoping the provider will solve the problem.

This hope is unfounded.

6.2 Stochastic Systems Produce Variance by Design

To understand why wrong answers are unavoidable, one must understand how LLMs work.

The Principle: Next-Token Prediction

An LLM was trained to predict the next word (more precisely: token). Given a context, it calculates probabilities for all possible next tokens.

Example:

Input: "The capital of France is"

The model calculates: - "Paris": 92% - "the": 3% - "a": 2% - "Lyon": 1% - Thousands of other tokens: each < 0.1%

Then it chooses. Not always the most probable. Otherwise every answer would be identical. It samples from the distribution—weighted by probability, but with a random component.

This is called "stochastic." The system rolls dice—with loaded dice, but it rolls.

Why This Produces Wrong Answers

Case 1: The correct answer is not the most probable

For trivial questions, the correct answer is usually also the most probable. "Capital of France" → "Paris."

For complex questions, not.

Question: "What is the maximum latency at 5 hops according to Document B?"

The model has no direct access to "Document B." It has probabilities derived from training data. If the most probable number is "50 ms" (because that appears in many similar documents), it says "50 ms"—even if the correct answer would be "325 ms."

Case 2: The question has no unambiguous answer

Question: "What risks exist in drone control?"

There is no single correct answer. There are many possible answers. The model generates a plausible one—which may omit important risks or emphasize unimportant ones.

Case 3: The model fills gaps

When the model cannot answer a question, it does not say "I don't know." It generates the most probable answer for this type of question.

The result: A fact-free but coherent answer. It sounds right. It reads right. It is wrong.

The Temperature Illusion

You can adjust the "temperature" of an LLM. Low temperature: less randomness, deterministic answers. High temperature: more creativity, more variance.

The illusion: "At temperature 0, the system is deterministic and makes no errors."

The reality: At temperature 0, the system always chooses the most probable token. This makes the answers predictable—not correct.

If the most probable answer is wrong, it is reliably wrong at temperature 0. Every time. Reproducibly.

6.3 Terminology: Honest Terms for the Phenomenon

If "hallucination" is the wrong term—what is the right one?

Proposal 1: Plausible Lie

Definition: An output that is linguistically correct, substantively plausible, but factually false.

Why fitting: - "Plausible" describes the quality: It sounds right - "Lie" describes the reality: It is false - No pathos, no disease metaphor

Example:

> Question: "When was the RTK-GPS module specified?"

> Answer: "The RTK-GPS module was specified in March 2024 (see Document A, page 47)."

Sounds precise. Contains source citation. But page 47 does not exist, and the date is invented.

This is not a hallucination. This is a plausible lie.

Proposal 2: Fact-Free but Coherent Answer

Definition: An output that is logically structured and linguistically flawless but has no connection to verifiable facts.

Why fitting: - Technically precise - No value judgment - Describes the phenomenon neutrally

Example:

> Question: "What security protocols apply to swarm communication?"

> Answer: "Swarm communication uses the XSP-7 protocol with 256-bit encryption, certified according to MIL-STD-882E."

Coherent. Detailed. Sounds like from a real document. "XSP-7" does not exist. The answer is invented—coherent but factless.

Proposal 3: Statistical Confabulation

Definition: An output generated from statistical patterns without access to the underlying facts.

Why fitting: - "Confabulation" is more precise than "hallucination" (describes filling of gaps) - "Statistical" points to the mechanism - Sounds technical, not pathological

Which Term to Use?

In this book: **Plausible lie** and **fact-free answer**.

Both terms make clear: The system functions as intended. It has no malfunction. It produces what it is supposed to produce—and that is not always the truth.

6.4 Implications for Contracts

The terminology has practical consequences.

With "Hallucination"

A provider could say: > "Our system has a hallucination rate of under 5%."

This implies: - There is a normal state (correct answers) - There is an error state (hallucinations) - The error state is rare and measurable - One can work to reduce it

This leads to expectations: - The provider will reduce the rate - At under 5%, you can trust the system - The 95% are reliable

With "Plausible Lie"

The same statement, different formulation: > "Our system produces plausible lies in about 5% of cases."

This implies: - Every answer can be a lie - You do not know beforehand which one - 5% is a lower bound, not a guarantee - Trust is not warranted

This leads to different expectations: - Every answer must be verified - Even the 95% can be wrong - The system does not replace expertise

The Legal Dimension

In contracts, the formulation makes a difference.

Variant A: > "The system is configured to minimize hallucinations."

This could be read as a commitment: The provider tries to reduce a defect.

Variant B: > "The system produces stochastic outputs. Factual correctness is architecturally not possible to guarantee."

This is a description: This is how the technology works.

Variant A invites warranty claims. Variant B excludes them.

Guess which variant appears in real contracts?

6.5 The Business Model Forces Answers

One last aspect: Why does the system not simply say "I don't know"?

The User Experience Problem

Imagine you use an AI assistant. You ask a question. The answer:
"I don't know."
You ask another question:
"I don't know."
A third question:
"I'm not sure."
How often do you pay for this service?

The business model of AI services is based on answers. A system that frequently says "I don't know" loses users. A system that always delivers a plausible answer—even if it is wrong—retains users.

Training Reinforces the Problem

LLMs are trained on human feedback (RLHF: Reinforcement Learning from Human Feedback). Humans prefer: - Answers over non-answers - Detailed answers over brief ones - Confident formulations over uncertain ones

The result: The model learns to always give an answer. Better a wrong answer than none.

The Uncertainty Illusion

Modern LLMs sometimes say "I'm not sure" or "possibly." This sounds like self-assessment.

It is not.

These phrases are trained. The model has learned that humans rate these hedges positively. It uses them when the statistical distribution is less clear—not when it "knows" that it does not know.

An LLM cannot know that it does not know. It has no model of its own limits. It has probabilities.

6.6 Key Points

- **"Hallucination" is the wrong term.** It suggests a malfunction. The system functions as intended.
- **Wrong answers are architecture-inherent.** Stochastic systems produce variance. This is not a bug, this is the principle.
- **Plausibility is not truth.** The model optimizes for probable outputs, not for correct ones.
- **Terminology determines expectation.** Those who say "hallucination" hope for a cure. Those who say "plausible lie" know that verification is necessary.
- **The business model forces answers.** A system that says "I don't know" loses customers. So, it answers—even when it does not know the answer.
- **Uncertainty signals are trained phrases.** "Possibly" does not mean the system knows its limits. It means the statistical distribution was less clear.
- **For contracts:** Fact-free answers are not defects. They are system properties.

The system functions as built. The question is: Who verifies whether what was built is correct? Chapter 7 examines the validation gap—the validator who cannot validate.

Chapter 7: The Validator Who Cannot Validate

Chapter 5 showed: Correctness cannot be guaranteed. Chapter 6 explained: Wrong answers are system-inherent.

Now the practical question: Who verifies?

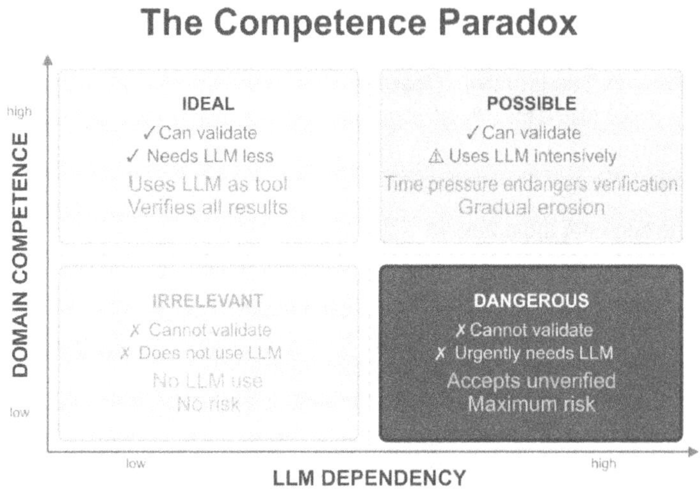

Figure 5 Those who have the competence to validate need the LLM less. Those who urgently need it cannot validate reliably. The most dangerous quadrant: high dependency with low competence.

7.1 Who Verifies Whether the LLM Is Right?

The LLM delivers an answer. Someone must decide whether the answer is correct.

Candidates:

Candidate	Can verify?	Problem
The LLM itself	No	No model of its own limits
A second LLM	No	Same architecture, same errors
The MSP	No	Does not know the domain
An algorithm	Partially	Only formal criteria verifiable
The domain expert	Yes	Must verify every answer

Only the domain expert remains. The human.

This is not a surprise. This is the core message of this book. But it has consequences that are rarely discussed.

7.2 The Engineer as Last Instance

Take the drone example.

The engineer asks the LLM: "Which latency assumptions in the communication protocol contradict the test protocols?"

The LLM answers:

"In Document A (page 47), a maximum latency of 75 ms is assumed. However, Test Protocol 23 (page 12) shows measured values of up to 325 ms under load. This constitutes a contradiction that could affect collision avoidance."

Sounds precise. Sounds helpful.

The engineer must now:

1. **Open Document A, page 47.** Does it really say "75 ms"? Or does it say "75–150 ms"? Or something else entirely?
2. **Check Test Protocol 23, page 12.** Are the "325 ms" correctly quoted? Under what conditions were they measured?
3. **Analyze the claimed contradiction.** Is it really a contradiction? Or are the 75 ms an average value and the 325 ms an extreme case?
4. **Check what is missing.** Did the LLM find all relevant documents? What about Document C, which uses "delay" instead of "latency"?

If the engineer does not perform this verification, he works with unverified assumptions. In a critical system.

If the engineer does perform this verification, he has done the work himself. The LLM gave him a starting point—nothing more.

The Time Calculation

Without LLM: - Search documents: 2 hours - Analyze contradictions: 1 hour - Document: 30 minutes - **Total: 3.5 hours**

With LLM: - Query LLM: 5 minutes - Verify source citations: 45 minutes - Analyze claimed contradictions: 1 hour - Check what is missing: 1 hour - Document: 30 minutes - **Total: 3 hours 20 minutes**

Savings: 10 minutes. Maybe.

And only if the LLM happened to find the right documents. If not, the search starts over—with the additional effort of untangling the false leads.

7.3 The Validation Gap

Forrester predicts for 2026 a "renaissance of human expertise" [Forrester 2025]. The reason: GenAI delivers "more information—or misinformation." Buyers turn to experts "to validate insights."

Forrester's recommendation: Enable employees to "identify bad results before they are implemented."

That sounds reasonable. It has just one catch.

The Gap

To identify bad results, you need: - Subject matter expertise - Time for verification - Access to original documents - The ability to recognize what is missing

> Those who have that need the LLM less.

An engineer who can judge whether "75 ms vs. 325 ms" is a real contradiction could also search the documents himself. He is the expert.

An engineer who cannot judge that also cannot validate the LLM answer. For him, the system is worthless—or dangerous.

The validation gap:

User Competence	Can Validate	Needs LLM
High (Expert)	Yes	Less
Medium (Professional)	Partially	With risk
Low (Layperson)	No	Not sensible at all

The LLM is most useful for those who can use it least safely.

The Assistance Paradox

An assistant is useful when he takes work off your hands.

An assistant whose work must be completely verified does not take work off your hands. He shifts it.

The Little Helper hands over the screw. The engineer checks the screw. The engineer could have gone to the drawer himself.

This works for simple tasks. For the tenth screw, or the hundredth, the assistant pays off.

For complex tasks—checking specifications, finding contradictions, assessing risks—every answer is unique. Every verification is new. Every validation costs.

7.4 What ISO 42001 Requires—And What It Leaves Open

ISO/IEC 42001:2023 is the first international standard for AI management systems. It addresses the validation question—but with telling vagueness.

The Relevant Clauses

Clause	Topic	Requirement
6.1.4	AI Risk Assessment	"The organization must identify risks from AI outputs"
8.4	Verification & Validation	"AI systems must be verified and validated before deployment"
9.1	Monitoring	"The organization must monitor the performance of the AI system"
A.6.2.4	Human Oversight	"Appropriate human oversight must be ensured"

This sounds reasonable. But let us look more closely.

The Vagueness by Example

ISO 42001, Clause 9.1 (paraphrased):

> *"The organization shall determine what needs to be monitored and measured, the methods for monitoring, measurement, analysis and evaluation, when the monitoring and measurement shall be performed, when the results shall be analyzed and evaluated."*

What the standard requires: A process must exist.

What the standard does not say: - Who specifically validates - What qualification this person needs - How much time must be planned for validation - What happens if no qualified person is available - How "sufficient" validation is defined

ISO 42001, Annex A.6.2.4 (Human Oversight):

> *"Controls should be implemented to ensure that AI system outputs are subject to appropriate human oversight."*

What the standard requires: "Appropriate" human oversight.

What the standard does not define: - What is "appropriate"? - For which outputs? - To what extent? - With what expertise?

The Certification Paradox

A company can be ISO 42001-certified and still perform no effective validation.

The auditor checks: "Do you have a documented process for validating AI outputs?"

The answer: "Yes. Here is the document."

That is sufficient for certification. Whether the process works—whether the right people with the right expertise check the right outputs—is a different question.

A Concrete Example

Process documentation (ISO 42001-compliant):

> *"AI-generated outputs are reviewed by a responsible employee before use. The review is documented in the ticket system."*

Reality:

The "responsible employee" is a junior developer. He has no drone expertise. He clicks "Reviewed" because the answer sounds plausible. The ticket is closed.

The standard is met. The validation did not take place.

What the Standard Cannot Accomplish

ISO 42001 is a management system standard. It defines that processes must exist. It cannot define whether these processes work substantively.

This is not a deficiency of the standard. It is a structural limit. A standard can require: "Validate." It cannot guarantee: "The validation is competent."

This guarantee requires: - Subject matter expertise in the company - Sufficient resources for validation - Honesty about one's own limits

No standard can enforce this. This is a leadership decision.

A Practical Example: Module Integration

The problem is not new. It already exists with traditional system integration.

The situation:

A company develops a complex system. Components from third-party suppliers are integrated. The engineers have manuals—hundreds of pages of supplier specifications.

The question: Do the specifications in the manual match reality?

The engineers' proposal:

"We should test the critical parameters in our own lab. The manuals describe ideal conditions. Our use case is different."

The engineers know: Manufacturer specifications are optimistic. Limits shift under load. Interactions between modules are not documented.

Management's decision:

"Too expensive. We trust the manuals. 80/20 rule: We only test the most important things."

The problem:

Which parameters belong to the 20% that must be tested? Which to the 80% that can be taken over?

Management does not know. It has no subject matter expertise in high-frequency technology, thermodynamics, or signal processing. It applies a heuristic without knowing what to.

The result:

The engineers shrug. They document their objection. They adopt the manufacturer specifications. The system is built.

Maybe it works. Maybe not. Maybe the error only shows years later, under conditions no one tested.

The parallel to LLMs:

With LLM outputs, the same thing happens—only faster and more frequently.

Traditional Integration	LLM Integration
Supplier manual	LLM output
"It's in the datasheet"	"The AI said so"
Engineer wants lab test	Engineer wants source verification
Management: "Too expensive"	Management: "Takes too long"
80/20 without knowing what's critical	"Most answers are correct anyway"

The pattern is identical: - The experts know validation is necessary - Management sees costs, not risks - The decision is against validation - No one knows which errors creep in

The difference:

With traditional integration, there is at least a datasheet you can sue over.

With LLM outputs, there is: "The provider assumes no warranty for substantive correctness."

The Lesson for Decision-Makers

This is not a new problem. Anyone who knows ISO 27001 (information security) knows the pattern.

An ISO 27001-certified company has: - Documented security policies - Defined responsibilities - Regular audits - Processes for incident response

An ISO 27001-certified company does not necessarily have: - Secure systems - Competent administrators - Current patches - Working backups

The certification says: "There is a process." It does not say: "The process protects you."

Numerous spectacular security incidents affected ISO 27001-certified companies. The certificate hung on the wall while the attackers were in the network.

ISO 42001 follows the same pattern:

ISO 27001	ISO 42001
Security processes documented	AI processes documented
"We have an ISMS"	"We have an AIMS"
Audit checks documents	Audit checks documents
Security not guaranteed	Quality not guaranteed

Those who commission an MSP that is "ISO 42001-certified" buy process documentation. They do not buy a quality guarantee.

ISO 42001 certification means: - There are documented processes - Risks have been identified - Responsibilities are assigned

ISO 42001 certification does not mean: - The processes work - The validation is accurate - The AI outputs are reliable

7.5 Why a Second LLM Does Not Solve the Problem

An obvious thought: Have a second LLM check the first one's answer.

The concept: 1. LLM A answers the question 2. LLM B checks A's answer 3. In case of contradiction: Escalation or third opinion

Why it does not work:

Reason 1: Same Architecture, Same Errors

Both LLMs are based on the same basic structure: Transformer, next-token prediction, stochastic outputs.

When LLM A produces a plausible lie, this lie is also plausible for LLM B. B was trained on similar data. B learned similar statistical patterns.

B says: "A's answer appears correct."

Two LLMs that confirm each other are not more reliable than one. They are just more expensive.

Reason 2: Correlated Errors

The training data overlaps. If the internet says the capital of Australia is Sydney, both models have learned that. Both will make the same error.

Diversity helps only with uncorrelated noise. With correlated noise, the problem doubles.

Reason 3: No Access to Truth

LLM B has no independent access to reality. It cannot read the original documents and compare with the answer. It can only judge whether the answer sounds plausible.

Plausibility is not a measure of truth. That was the topic of Chapter 6.

Reason 4: Infinite Regress

If B checks A's answer—who checks B?

A third LLM? Who checks the third?

In the end, you need a human who decides. Then this human can also directly check A's answer.

The "Validator Tower"

Some providers build complex pipelines: - LLM for research - LLM for summarization - LLM for quality checking - LLM for formatting

This is impressive. It does not solve the problem.

Each stage can introduce errors. No stage can reliably detect errors. The tower becomes taller but not more stable.

7.6 What Can Be Automatically Verified

Not everything is hopeless. Some aspects can be automatically verified.

Verifiable:

Criterion	Method	Example
Syntactic correctness	Parser	Code compiles
Format	Schema validation	JSON is valid
Source citation present	Pattern matching	"Page X" is contained
No forbidden terms	Word list	No competitor products mentioned
Length	Character count	< 500 words

Not verifiable:

Criterion	Problem
Source citation correct	Requires document access + understanding
Substantively correct	Requires domain expertise
Complete	Requires knowing what is missing
Consistent with other documents	Requires overall context
Suitable for purpose	Requires understanding the purpose

The important criteria are not automatically verifiable. They require human judgment.

7.7 The Organizational Consequence

What does this mean for companies?

Scenario 1: LLM Without Validation

The company deploys an LLM. The outputs are used directly.

Result: - Fast processing - Unknown error rate - Risk in critical decisions - Eventually: the first damage

Scenario 2: LLM With Complete Validation

Every LLM output is checked by a domain expert.

Result: - High quality - High effort - Questionable efficiency - The question: Why not just do it yourself?

Scenario 3: LLM With Selective Validation

Some outputs are checked, others are not. By importance, risk, availability.

Result: - Compromise between effort and risk - Processes needed: Who decides what is checked? - The unchecked outputs remain risky - Documentation obligation: What was checked, what was not?

The Honest Recommendation

For critical applications—drone specifications, medical documentation, legal research—there is no shortcut.

Either you verify. Or you accept the risk.

"AI saves time" is only true if verification is omitted. If it is omitted, the system is not safe. If it is not omitted, the time savings are minimal.

This is uncomfortable. It is reality.

7.8 Key Points

- The domain expert is the last instance. No technology replaces human judgment in validation.
- Validation costs. Time, expertise, attention. The costs are often higher than the claimed savings.
- The validation gap is structural. Those who can validate need the LLM less. Those who need it cannot safely validate.
- ISO 42001 requires processes, not competence. A certified company has documented procedures. Whether they work is another question.
- Two LLMs are not better than one. Same architecture, correlated errors, no access to truth.
- Automatically verifiable: form. Syntax, format, length—yes. Substantive correctness—no.
- Forrester is right: The "renaissance of human expertise" is coming. Not as regression but as necessity.

- For critical applications: Either verify or accept risk. There is no shortcut.

The validation gap cannot be closed. But what does this mean for the managed service contract? Chapter 8 examines the paradox: Responsibility without insight—Managed Service without access.

Chapter 8: Managed Service Without Access

The previous chapters have shown: - Correctness cannot be guaranteed (Chapter 5) - Wrong answers are system-inherent (Chapter 6) - Validation requires domain expertise (Chapter 7)

Now the contractual consequence: What happens when you try to define a managed service for something the service provider is not allowed to see?

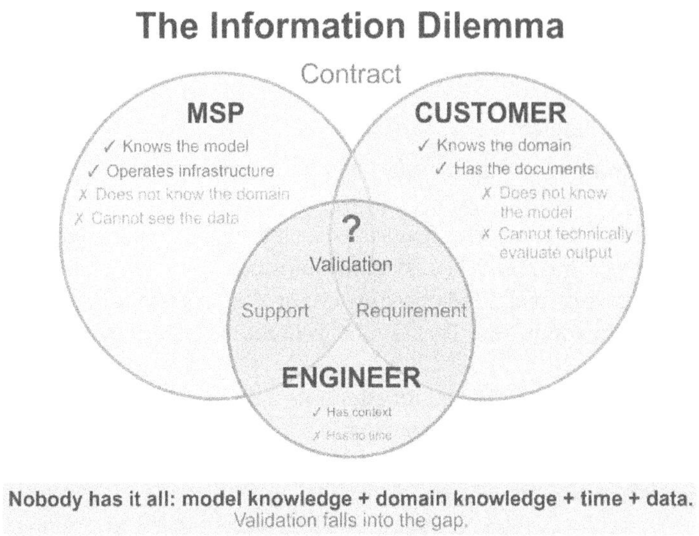

Figure 6 Nobody has it all: model knowledge + domain knowledge + time + data. Validation falls into the gap.

8.1 What the Service Provider Is Not Allowed to See

Back to the drone example.

A company develops drone swarms. The documentation includes:

Technical specifications: - Communication protocols - Encryption methods - Collision avoidance algorithms - Swarm coordination logic

Trade secrets: - Optimization procedures (competitive advantage) - Energy management algorithms - Proprietary sensor integration

Regulatory-sensitive information: - Dual-use relevant technologies - Export-controlled components - Security certifications

These documents cannot be given to an external service provider. Not from distrust. For legal reasons.

The Confidentiality Pyramid

Level	Example	Transfer to MSP
Public	Product brochure	Yes
Internal	Project plans	Possible with NDA
Confidential	Technical specifications	Problematic
Strictly confidential	Algorithms, encryption	No
Regulated	Dual-use, export control	Prohibited

An LLM for document analysis needs access to the documents. Precisely to those that must not be released.

The NDA Problem

"We sign an NDA. Then it's safe."

No.

An NDA regulates what happens when information is misused. It does not prevent misuse. It creates claims afterward.

For trade secrets: The damage has occurred as soon as the information is with the competitor. The NDA helps in court. It does not help in the market.

For export-controlled information: The transfer itself can be criminal. An NDA changes nothing about that.

For dual-use technologies: The authorities are not interested in NDAs between private companies.

8.2 What the Service Provider Cannot Maintain

Suppose the confidentiality problem could be solved. The MSP gets access to the documents.

What can he do with them?

The Maintenance Illusion

With classic server hosting, the MSP "maintains": - Install updates - Monitor logs - Fix errors - Optimize performance

This works because the MSP understands the technology. Servers are servers. The problems are known.

With an LLM system for drone development, the MSP would have to:

- Check whether the answers are substantively correct
- Understand what "Latency 75 ms vs. 325 ms" means

- Recognize when relevant documents are not found
- Judge whether an alleged contradiction is actually one

For that, he needs drone expertise. He does not have it. He cannot have it—not for this customer and simultaneously for the medical technology customer and the automotive customer.

The Economies of Scale Illusion

The point of managed service is scaling: One expert serves many customers.

This works with standardized technology:

- Windows servers: same for every customer
- Network monitoring: same tools, same metrics
- Backup management: same processes

It does not work with substantive validation:

- Drone specifications: unique
- Medical device documentation: unique
- Legal text analysis: unique

Each domain needs its own expertise. There are no economies of scale.

What the MSP Can Actually Maintain

Task	MSP Can	MSP Cannot
Server runs	✓	
API responds	✓	
Model loaded	✓	
Answer generated	✓	
Answer correct		X
Nothing overlooked		X
Substantively appropriate		X

The MSP can maintain infrastructure. He cannot maintain quality.

8.3 The Contract No One Wants to Write

Let us try to formulate an honest contract.

Contract Draft A: Honest but Unsaleable

Service Description:

The service provider provides infrastructure for operating an LLM system. The service provider warrants:

- Availability of infrastructure (99.5%)
- Technical support for system outages
- Regular security updates

Exclusions:

The service provider does not warrant:

- The substantive correctness of system outputs
- The completeness of research results
- Suitability for specific application purposes
- Consistency with source documents

Customer Responsibility:

The customer is responsible for:

- Validating all system outputs before use
- Providing qualified personnel for verification
- The decision to use outputs
- All consequences from using outputs

This is honest. It describes what the MSP can deliver.

It is unsaleable. No customer pays €144,000 per year for a service that explicitly says: "You are responsible for what matters."

Contract Draft B: Saleable but Dishonest

Service Description:

The service provider operates an AI-powered document analysis system. The system enables:

- Intelligent document search
- Automatic contradiction detection
- AI-powered summaries

Service Level:

- Availability: 99.5%
- Response time: < 2 seconds
- Support: 24/7

Quality Assurance:

The service provider employs state-of-the-art quality assurance methods. The system is continuously optimized.
This is saleable. It sounds like value.

It is dishonest. The "quality assurance" refers to technical quality. The "state-of-the-art methods" are availability monitoring. The "continuous optimization" is model updates.

None of this guarantees that the answers are correct.

The Reality

Most contracts lie between A and B. They hide the exclusions in the fine print. They emphasize the technical services. They leave open who is liable for substantive errors.

This is not a coincidence. It is the only way to close a contract.

An honest contract would find no buyer. A dishonest contract would ruin the provider as soon as the first damage occurs.

So you write something in between and hope it goes well.

8.4 The Paradox: Responsibility Without Insight

Now the paradox becomes visible.

The Customer's Position

The customer:

- Needs support with document analysis
- Cannot or does not want to build the competence himself
- Hopes the MSP solves the problem
- Signs a contract that leaves him with the responsibility

The customer buys a service hoping to hand off responsibility. The contract says: The responsibility stays with you.

The MSP's Position

The MSP:

- Can operate infrastructure
- Cannot see the documents (confidentiality)
- Cannot judge quality (domain expertise)
- Cannot assume responsibility (liability risk)

The MSP sells a service knowing it does not solve the core problem. He hopes the customer does not notice what he is not getting.

The Engineer's Position

The engineer (at the customer):

- Knows validation is necessary
- Has no time for complete validation
- Is supposed to trust the system because management bought it
- Bears the professional responsibility for the result

The engineer is caught in the middle. He is supposed to use a system he cannot trust. He is supposed to take responsibility for results he has not verified. He is supposed to become more productive even though he would need to verify more.

> **The Paradox in One Sentence**
> The MSP has the technology but not the insight. The customer has the responsibility but not the competence. The engineer has the competence but not the time. No one has everything that would be necessary.

8.5 The Consequence for Critical Applications

For non-critical applications, this can work:

- Marketing texts: Errors are embarrassing, not dangerous
- Internal summaries: Will be revised anyway
- Idea generation: Wrong ideas are discarded

For critical applications, it does not work: - Drone specifications: Errors lead to crashes - Medical documentation: Errors endanger patients - Legal analysis: Errors lead to liability

The boundary runs where "wrong" has consequences that go beyond correction.

The Uncomfortable Truth

For critical applications, there is no functioning managed service for LLMs.

Not because the technology is bad. Not because the providers are incapable. But because the structure of the problem does not allow it.

An LLM produces stochastic outputs. Validation requires domain expertise. The MSP does not have this expertise. The customer has it—or no one does.

If the customer has it, he does not need the service as much. If he does not have it, he cannot use the service safely.

This is the Little Helper Paradox in its contractual form.

8.6 Key Points

- **Confidentiality prevents access.** The most important documents cannot be released. The MSP is supposed to maintain what he is not allowed to see.
- **Domain expertise prevents scaling.** Each domain needs its own knowledge. There are no economies of scale in substantive validation.
- **The honest contract is not an attractive sell.** Those who explicitly say what they cannot deliver find no customers.
- **The contract that is an attractive sell is dishonest.** Those who conceal what they cannot deliver risk liability and reputation.
- **The paradox remains unsolvable:** The MSP has technology without insight. The customer has responsibility without competence. The engineer has competence without time.
- **For critical applications:** There is no functioning managed service for LLMs. The structure of the problem prevents it.

Part 2 "The Falsification" is complete. The promise was tested and falsified. Part 3 examines the consequences: What does this mean for liability, for insurance, for the sensible use of LLMs?

Part 3: The Consequences

Chapter 9: Legal Classification—Civil Law Meets AI

The falsification is complete. Part 2 showed: AI as managed service for critical applications does not work structurally.

Part 3 asks: What does this mean legally? Who is liable when things go wrong? And what rules apply at all?

The answer is more complicated than one hopes.

9.1 Introduction: Stochastic Systems in the Legal Framework

The law is built for deterministic systems.

A car drives or does not drive. A contract is fulfilled or not fulfilled. A product is defective or defect-free.

An LLM is different. It produces outputs that: - Are sometimes correct - Are sometimes wrong - Are never predictable - Always sound plausible

The law knows "defective" and "defect-free." It does not know "statistically mostly correct."

The Three Legal Levels

Level	Regulation	Focus
National	Civil Code (e.g., German BGB §§ 327 ff.)	Contract law, digital products
EU	AI Act (Regulation 2024/1689)	Product safety, market surveillance
EU	Product Liability Directive (2024/2853)	Strict liability

Additionally, there are standards like ISO 42001, which are not legal norms but can define standards of care.

Each level has gaps. Together, they form a regulatory framework with considerable uncertainties.

Note for international readers: While this chapter references the German Civil Code (BGB), similar principles apply in most jurisdictions. The EU AI Act and Product Liability Directive apply throughout the European Union. The structural problems described—how law designed for deterministic systems struggles with stochastic ones—are universal.

9.2 The Civil Law Problem: Where AI Does Not Fit

Since January 2022, §§ 327–327u of the German Civil Code (BGB) regulate "contracts for digital products." This covers digital content and digital services.

An LLM service is a digital service. So the rules apply. Theoretically.

Subjective Requirements

> *"The digital product must meet the subjective requirements."*

Subjective requirements are what was contractually agreed.

With traditional software:

- Agreed: "The program calculates income tax."
- Delivered: The program calculates income tax.
- Verifiable: Input €5,000, expected output €X.

With an LLM:

- Agreed: "The system answers questions about documents."
- Delivered: The system answers questions about documents.
- Verifiable: ???

The system answers. But are the answers "correct"? What does "correct" mean for a summary? For a contradiction analysis?

The subjective requirements are met as soon as the system answers. That the answers can be wrong is—as Chapter 6 showed—not a defect but a system property.

Objective Requirements

> "The digital product must meet the objective requirements."

Objective requirements include:

- Suitability for ordinary use
- Customary quality
- What the consumer can expect

The problem:

What is the "customary quality" of an LLM?

- That it answers? Yes.
- That it sometimes answers incorrectly? Also yes.
- That the user must verify? Apparently also yes.

The "customary quality" of an LLM includes wrong answers. They are not unusual—they are normal.

A buyer who buys an LLM and receives wrong answers gets exactly what is customary.

Update Obligation

"The entrepreneur must provide updates that are necessary to maintain conformity."

With traditional software: Security updates, bug fixes, compatibility updates.

With an LLM:

Which update fixes the problem that the model gives wrong answers?

- A new model? That also gives wrong answers. Different ones, but wrong.
- Better training? Shifts the errors, does not eliminate them.
- More parameters? No guarantee of fewer errors.

The update obligation runs empty. There is no update that makes a stochastic system deterministic.

Reversal of Burden of Proof

"If a defect appears within one year of delivery, it is presumed that the digital product was already defective at delivery."

This is consumer-friendly. With traditional software.

With an LLM:

- Day 1: The system answers Question X correctly.
- Day 100: The system answers Question X incorrectly.

Is this a defect that "already existed at delivery"?

No. The system was just as stochastic on Day 1 as on Day 100. It just got lucky. The reversal of burden of proof leads nowhere because there is no state to prove.

9.3 The EU AI Act: Rules Before Damage

Regulation (EU) 2024/1689—the "AI Act"—has been in force since August 1, 2024. It takes a different approach than contract law: not contract law but product safety.

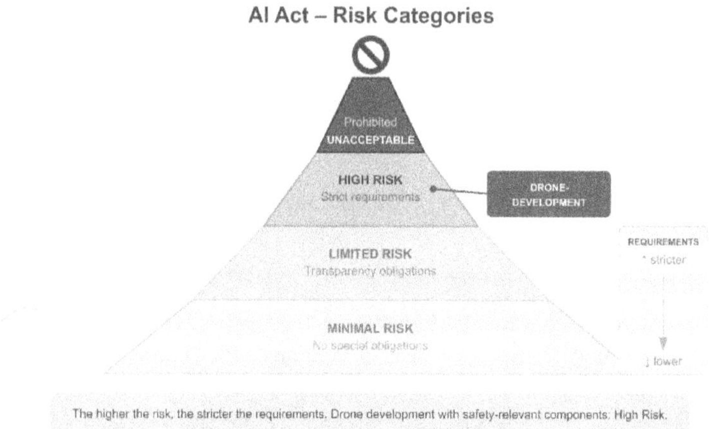

Figure 7 The AI Act risk pyramid: The higher the risk, the stricter the requirements. Drone development with safety-relevant components falls into the high-risk category.

The Risk Classes

Class	Examples	Consequence
Unacceptable	Social scoring, manipulative AI	Prohibited
High-risk	Medical devices, critical infrastructure, safety components	Strict obligations
Limited	Chatbots, deepfakes	Transparency obligations
Minimal	Spam filters, recommendation systems	No specific obligations

Drone Development = High-Risk

According to Annex III of the AI Act, "high-risk" includes among others: "AI systems intended to be used as safety components in the management and operation of critical digital infrastructure [...]"
And:

"AI systems intended to be used as safety components in the development, operation or control of machinery covered by Regulation (EU) 2023/1230 [Machinery Regulation]."

Drone swarms are machinery. An LLM that helps with specification review is a safety component—if its outputs flow into development.

The consequence: High-risk requirements.

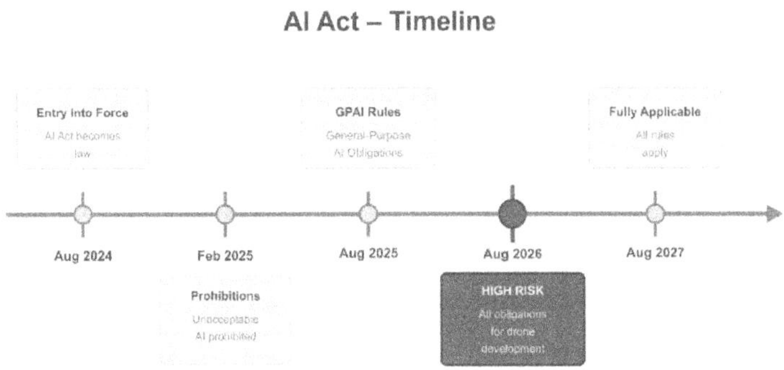

Figure 8 The AI Act timeline: Phased implementation from August 2024 to August 2027. High-risk obligations for drone development apply from August 2026.

The Timeline

Date	What Applies
August 1, 2024	AI Act in force
February 2, 2025	Prohibitions for unacceptable AI
August 2, 2025	GPAI rules (General Purpose AI)
August 2, 2026	High-risk obligations fully applicable

We are writing January 2026. The GPAI rules apply. The high-risk obligations take full effect in seven months.

9.4 Human Oversight (Art. 14 AI Act)

Article 14 is central to our topic:

> *"High-risk AI systems shall be designed and developed [...] in such a way that they can be effectively overseen by natural persons."*

Specifically, Art. 14 requires:

- The oversight person must understand the system's capabilities and limitations
- They must be able to correctly interpret the outputs
- They must be able to decide not to use or to override the system
- They must be able to recognize signs of anomalies

The problem:

Art. 14 demands exactly what Chapter 7 described as impossible.

- "Correctly interpret outputs" → requires domain expertise
- "Understand capabilities and limitations" → not fully possible with stochastic systems
- "Recognize anomalies" → How do you recognize that a plausible lie is a lie?

The AI Act requires effective human oversight. It does not say how this should work with systems that do not mark their errors as errors.

9.5 The CLOUD Act—When EU Law Is Not Enough

The AI Act regulates much. It does not regulate what happens when US law crosses EU law.

Max Schrems and the Elephant in the Room

The Austrian privacy activist Max Schrems has won twice before the European Court of Justice:

- **Schrems I (2015):** Safe Harbor struck down
- **Schrems II (2020):** Privacy Shield struck down

The reason was the same each time: US surveillance laws are incompatible with EU fundamental rights. US intelligence agencies have access to data at US companies—without EU citizens having effective legal recourse.

In 2023 came the **EU-US Data Privacy Framework**—the third attempt. Schrems has already announced he will challenge this one too. The fundamental problem persists.

The CLOUD Act 2018

The Clarifying Lawful Overseas Use of Data Act (CLOUD Act) of 2018 clarifies:

US authorities can demand that US companies hand over data—regardless of where that data is stored.

This means: - Microsoft must hand over data, even if it is stored in Frankfurt - Amazon must hand over data, even if it is stored in Dublin - Every US company worldwide is affected - Every subsidiary of a US company is affected

What This Means for Customers

The AI Act protects data within EU jurisdiction. The CLOUD Act punctures this protection for all customers whose data is with US providers.

The chain:

1. German drone company uses "AI as a Service"
2. The MSP operates on Azure, AWS, or Google Cloud
3. Or: The MSP uses OpenAI/Anthropic API in the backend
4. A US National Security Letter arrives
5. The 2,000 pages of drone specification go to a US agency
6. The German customer does not learn about it (Gag Order possible)
7. The EU AI Act did not prevent this

The affected providers:

Provider	Headquarters	CLOUD Act
Microsoft Azure	USA	Yes
Amazon AWS	USA	Yes
Google Cloud	USA	Yes
OpenAI	USA	Yes
Anthropic	USA	Yes
Deutsche Telekom	Germany	No
OVHcloud	France	No
IONOS	Germany	No

But caution: Even a German MSP that uses US cloud services brings its customers' data within the reach of the CLOUD Act.

Particularly Critical: Dual-Use and Export Control

Drone development is often dual-use—usable for civilian and military purposes. This draws strategic interest.

In addition to the CLOUD Act:

- **ITAR** (International Traffic in Arms Regulations): US export control for defense goods
- **EAR** (Export Administration Regulations): US export control for dual-use

Those who incorporate components of US origin or use US technology may be subject to US jurisdiction—even as a German company.

The question is not only: "Can the MSP see my data?" The question is also: "Can the US government see my data?"

The Gag Order

Particularly insidious: US authorities can impose a Gag Order. The US provider may then not even disclose that a request has been made.
The German customer:

- Does not know that their data was requested
- Cannot defend themselves - Cannot take countermeasures
- May never find out

The Question for Management

Anyone commissioning a managed service for AI should ask:

"Where is my data physically located? Which law does it fall under? What US connections does the provider or its infrastructure have?"

The answer "GDPR-compliant" is not enough. The answer "Servers in Frankfurt" is not enough if the operator is a US company.

For critical applications—drones, medical technology, defense suppliers—this is not a theoretical question. It is a question of due diligence.

What the AI Act Does Not Regulate

The AI Act requires: - Data protection (Art. 10) - Cybersecurity (Art. 15) - Documentation (Art. 11)

The AI Act does not regulate: - Protection from non-European government access - Obligation to use EU-based providers - Disclosure obligation for US jurisdiction

This is a deliberate gap. An EU regulation cannot override US law. It can only—through strict localization requirements—limit the scope of application.

These requirements are largely missing. The market is open to US providers. With all the consequences this entails.

9.6 Data Governance (Art. 10 AI Act)

Article 10 regulates the quality of training data:

"Training, validation and testing data sets shall be subject to appropriate data governance measures."

This includes: - Document relevant design decisions - Check data sets for gaps and deficiencies - Identify possible biases

The problem for managed services:

Those who use a pre-trained model (such as Llama or Mistral) have no influence on the training data. They do not know what was in the training. They cannot fulfill Art. 10.

The AI Act distinguishes between "Provider" (who develops the system) and "Deployer" (who uses it). The data governance obligations primarily apply to the Provider.

But: If the Deployer modifies the system (fine-tuning, RAG with own data), they may themselves become a Provider. With all obligations this involves.

9.7 Post-Market Monitoring (Art. 72 AI Act)

Article 72 obligates providers of high-risk AI systems:

> *"To establish, document and maintain a post-market monitoring system."*

The system must: - Collect data about performance - Detect serious incidents - Enable corrective measures

With traditional software: Collect error reports, analyze crashes, distribute patches.

With an LLM: What is a "serious incident"?

- The system crashes → clear.
- The system gives a wrong answer → serious?
- The wrong answer leads to a wrong decision → when does the provider learn about it?
- The wrong decision leads to damage → months later, if at all.

Post-market monitoring for LLMs is conceptually unclear. Wrong answers are not a bug you can patch. They are system behavior.

9.8 GPAI Special Rules Since August 2025

Since August 2, 2025, special rules apply for "General Purpose AI"—that is, models like GPT, Claude, Llama that can be used for many purposes.

Obligations for All GPAI Providers

- Create technical documentation
- Provide information for downstream providers
- Comply with copyright rules
- Publish a summary of the training data

Additional Obligations for "Systemic Risk"

Models with particularly high capability (threshold: 10^25 FLOP in training) are subject to additional obligations:

- Conduct model evaluation
- Assess and mitigate systemic risks
- Report serious incidents
- Ensure adequate cybersecurity

The relevance for managed services:

Those who deploy a GPAI model in a high-risk application must ensure that the provider has fulfilled their obligations. The Deployer is indirectly affected.

An MSP that operates an open-source model must check: Has the original provider fulfilled the GPAI obligations? Is the required documentation available?

9.9 The Liability Gap: AI Act Defines Obligations, Not Liability

The AI Act defines obligations. It does not define liability.

Art. 99 regulates sanctions: Fines up to 35 million euros or 7% of global annual turnover.

But: These are public law sanctions. The state punishes violations.

What the AI Act does not regulate:

- Who is liable under civil law when an AI system causes damage?
- Who bears the burden of proof?
- What claims does the injured party have?

These questions were supposed to be answered by the "AI Liability Directive"—a directive proposal from the Commission in 2022.

Status: Withdrawn.

In February 2025, the proposal was withdrawn. The member states could not agree. Too many interests, too many open questions.

The consequence:

The AI Act creates obligations. It does not create clear liability. Those damaged by an AI system must fall back on national liability rules—which were written for deterministic systems.

9.10 Product Liability Directive 2024/2853

The new Product Liability Directive (PLD) was adopted in October 2024. It applies from December 9, 2026.

What Changes

Old (1985)	New (2024)
Only physical products	Also software
Only personal injury and property damage	Also data loss
No AI specifics	Explicit AI rules

Software as Product

Art. 4 defines:

> *"'Product' means any movable item, even if integrated into another movable or into an immovable item, including electricity and digital building files, as well as software."*

An LLM is software. An LLM is a product. Product liability applies.

Strict Liability

Product liability is strict liability. The manufacturer is liable if the product is defective—regardless of whose fault it is.

The problem:

When is an LLM "defective"?

Art. 6 of the Directive defines:

"A product is defective if it does not provide the safety a person is entitled to expect."

What does a person expect from an LLM?

- That it answers? ✓
- That the answers are correct? May they expect that?

If the market communicates: "LLMs can give wrong answers"—and every provider has corresponding disclaimers—then the wrong answer is not a deviation from legitimate expectations.

The system does what it is supposed to. It just does not do it reliably.

Reversal of Burden of Proof for Injured Parties

Art. 9 introduces evidentiary facilitations:

> *"If the claimant [...] demonstrates with a preponderance of probability that the product was defective or that the defectiveness of the product is a probable cause of the damage, the defectiveness of the product shall be presumed to be established."*

This helps affected parties—if they can prove that a defect existed.

With an LLM:

- The answer was wrong → provable
- The answer was "defective" in the sense of product liability law → unclear
- The defectiveness was causal → the engineer trusted the answer?

The reversal of burden of proof helps when it is clear what a defect is. With stochastic systems, it is not clear.

9.11 ISO 42001: AI Management System

Chapter 7 already critically examined ISO 42001. Here, we discuss the legal classification.

Not a Law, but Relevant

ISO 42001 is not a law. The standard is voluntary. No one has to be certified.

But:

- Courts can use ISO standards as "state of the art"
- Insurers can require or reward certification
- The AI Act refers to "harmonized standards" (Art. 40–41)
- Customers can require certification as an award criterion

Those who are not certified must explain in a dispute why their measures are equivalent.

The Limits of the Standard

As shown in Chapter 7:

ISO 42001 requires processes. It does not guarantee quality.

A certified company has documented procedures. Whether these procedures solve the problem—whether the right people with the right expertise check the right outputs—the certificate does not say.

For managed services:

"ISO 42001-certified" is a sales argument. It is not a liability waiver. It is no guarantee that validation works.

9.12 The Triple Gap

Let us summarize. The legal system has three gaps:

Gap 1: Civil Law Does Not Fit

Contract law for digital products assumes deterministic systems.

- Subjective requirements: met when the system answers
- Objective requirements: wrong answers are "customary"
- Update obligation: there is no update against stochasticity
- Reversal of burden of proof: no state to prove

Consequence: Warranty claims for wrong LLM answers are legally unclear.

Gap 2: The AI Act Defines No Liability

The AI Act creates obligations: Documentation, oversight, monitoring.

It creates no civil liability. The AI Liability Directive was withdrawn.

Consequence: Those damaged by an AI system have no clear path to claims.

Gap 3: Product Liability Does Not Quite Apply

The new Product Liability Directive covers software.

But: An LLM that gives wrong answers may not be "defective" in the legal sense—if wrong answers correspond to legitimate expectations.

Consequence: Product liability claims for LLM errors are also unclear.

The Overall Picture

Question	Civil Law	AI Act	Product Liability
Is wrong answer a defect?	Unclear	N/A	Unclear
Who is liable for damage?	Unclear	Not regulated	Provider, but...
Burden of proof on injured party?	Reversed, but for what?	N/A	Facilitated, but for what?
Can you protect yourself?	Contractually limited	Compliance helps	Unclear

9.13 What This Means for Contracts

For the Provider

The provider of an LLM managed service faces a dilemma:

Option A: Assume no liability

> *"No liability is assumed for substantive correctness."*

This is honest. It may also be effective—at least in B2B, where liability exclusions are easier to enforce.

But it makes the service unattractive. Who pays for something that explicitly does not guarantee?

Option B: Assume liability

This would be commercially attractive. It would also be ruinous at the first major damage.

No reasonable provider assumes liability for the substantive correctness of LLM outputs.

For the Customer

The customer must understand:

1. **The contract does not protect them.** The standard clauses exclude substantive liability.
2. **The law barely protects them.** The legal situation is unclear. A lawsuit would be lengthy and expensive.

3. **The responsibility stays with them.** Deployer obligations under AI Act, validation obligation in practice.

For the Engineer

The engineer bears the operational risk:

- They use the system
- They trust (or distrust) the outputs
- They bear the professional responsibility
- They may be personally liable (professional regulations, organizational negligence)

The system does not relieve them. It burdens them additionally—with the duty to verify what is barely verifiable.

9.14 Key Points

- **Civil law does not fit stochastic systems.** Warranty, update obligation, and reversal of burden of proof are designed for deterministic products.
- **The AI Act creates obligations, not liability.** Providers and Deployers have obligations. Who is liable for violations remains unclear.
- **The AI Liability Directive is missing.** The proposal was withdrawn. The liability gap remains.
- **The CLOUD Act punctures EU protection.** Data at US providers is subject to US jurisdiction—even with servers in the EU. Max Schrems has brought this problem to the ECJ twice.
- **Customers are directly affected.** Those who process confidential data at US providers risk access by US authorities—without knowing about it (Gag Order).
- **The Product Liability Directive helps conditionally.** Software is covered. But is a wrong LLM answer a “defect”?
- **Art. 14 AI Act requires effective oversight.** The law does not say how this works with systems that do not mark their errors.
- **ISO 42001 is not a shield.** Certification shows processes. It does not guarantee quality.
- **For critical applications:** Ask not only “Who can see my data?” but also “Which law does it fall under?”
- **For contracts:** Providers do not assume liability for content. Customers bear responsibility. Engineers bear risk.

The legal situation is unclear. But eventually there will be damage. Chapter 10 plays through the scenario: The drone crashes. Who is liable?

Chapter 10: The Liability Chain to Nowhere

Chapter 9 described the legal situation: Civil law does not fit, the AI Act does not regulate liability, product liability does not quite apply.

Now, we get into the concrete side of things. What happens when something goes wrong?

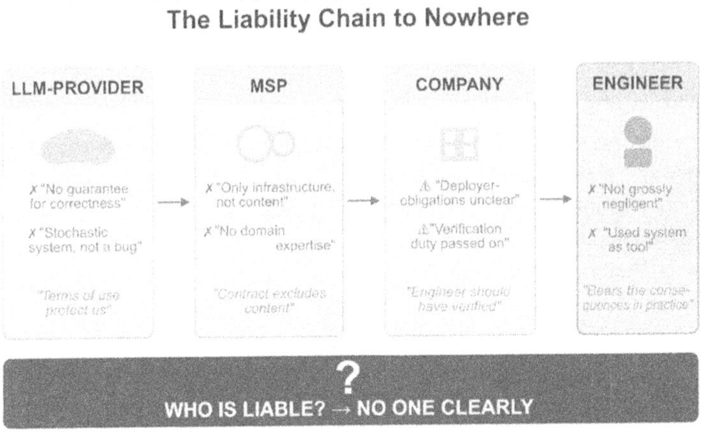

Figure 9 From the LLM provider through the managed service provider to the company and the individual engineer – everyone has a plausible defense. No one is clearly liable.

10.1 The Drone Scenario Played Through

Let us walk through the case. Step by step.

The Starting Point

A mid-sized company develops drone swarms for inspection tasks. 2,000 pages of specifications. Dozens of subsystems. Hundreds of interfaces.

The company uses a managed service for AI-powered document analysis. The service promises:

- “Intelligent research in your documents”
- “Automatic contradiction detection”
- “AI-powered quality assurance”

The contract says (in the fine print): - “No liability is assumed for substantive correctness” - “Use at own risk” - “Verification by customer required”

The Error

An engineer asks the system: "What latency assumptions apply to swarm communication?"

The system answers:

"According to the communication specification (Document K-2024-07, page 34), the maximum latency is 50 ms. This value is consistent with the requirements for collision avoidance."

The engineer adopts the value. He has no time to check all 2,000 pages. The system provided a source. The formulation sounds confident.

The Reality

In Document K-2024-07, page 34, it actually says "50 ms"—but as an average value under laboratory conditions.

In Document T-2024-03 (test protocols) it says: "Under load, latencies up to 325 ms were measured."

In Document A-2023-11 (architecture decisions) it says: "Collision avoidance assumes maximum latency of 75 ms."

The LLM found one document and cited it. It did not find the others—or did not classify them as relevant. It did not recognize the contradiction.

The Damage

The drone is specified with the wrong latency assumption. Collision avoidance fails under real conditions. During a test flight, a drone crashes. Property damage: €180,000. Fortunately, there were no personal injuries.

Who is liable?

10.2 The Liability Candidates

Candidate 1: The LLM Provider

The provider developed the model. Trained it. Brought it to market.

Arguments for liability:

- The model produced a wrong answer
- The provider chose the architecture
- The provider advertises "intelligence" and "reliability"

Arguments against liability:

- The model functioned as designed (stochastic outputs)
- The provider made no commitment to substantive correctness
- The terms of use exclude liability for content
- The provider did not know what the model was being used for

Legal classification:

Under the new Product Liability Directive (Directive (EU) 2024/2853, PLD), software is a product. But is a wrong answer a "defect"?

Art. 6 PLD defines: A product is defective if it does not provide the safety a person is entitled to expect.

What may one expect from an LLM? That it answers—yes. That the answers are correct—may one expect that when every provider explicitly warns against it?

Probable outcome: Provider liability unlikely. The warnings and terms of use should provide protection.

Candidate 2: The Managed Service Provider (MSP)

The MSP operated the system. Made it available to the customer. Took money for it.

Arguments for liability: - The MSP sold a service - The MSP committed to availability and support - The MSP implicitly promised utility

Arguments against liability: - The MSP explicitly excluded substantive correctness - The MSP cannot assess the domain (drone development) - The MSP delivered technically flawlessly (system ran, answer was generated) - The contract places verification obligation on the customer

Legal classification:

The MSP contract is a service contract. The service was: Provision of a functioning system. The system functioned.

The service was not: Guarantee for correct answers. That is explicitly not in the contract.

Probable outcome: MSP liability unlikely. The contract is on their side.

Candidate 3: The Company (Deployer)

The company deployed the system. Made the decision to use AI for critical tasks.

Arguments for liability: - The company selected the system - The company defined the processes - The company assumed the verification obligation (per contract) - The company is the "Deployer" in the sense of the AI Act

Arguments against liability: - The company trusted the MSP - The company acted in good faith - Resources for full verification were lacking

Legal classification:

Under the AI Act, the Deployer has obligations (Art. 26): - Ensure input data is relevant - Monitor system performance - Suspend use in case of risks

Did the company fulfill these obligations? Hard to say. The obligations are vaguely formulated.

Probable outcome: The company will bear part of the responsibility. It deployed the system and assumed the contractual verification obligation.

Candidate 4: The Engineer

The engineer adopted the LLM answer. Did not verify. Released the wrong specification.

Arguments for liability: - The engineer is a professional - The engineer should have verified - The engineer bears professional responsibility

Arguments against liability: - The engineer used an approved tool - Verifying all 2,000 pages was not realistic - Management mandated the system - The engineer did not sign a personal assumption of liability

Legal classification:

Employees are liable for damages only in cases of intent or gross negligence. Was it grossly negligent to trust an LLM answer with a source citation?

That is the central question. And it is not answered.

Probable outcome: Personal liability of the engineer is unlikely—unless gross negligence is present. But where the boundary lies is unclear.

10.3 The Responsibility Gap

Let us summarize:

Actor	Probably Liable?	Why Not?
LLM Provider	No	Terms of use, no "defect" in legal sense
MSP	No	Contract excludes substantive liability
Company	Partially	Assumed verification obligation, but obligations unclear
Engineer	Unlikely	Employee liability only for gross negligence

The result: €180,000 in damage. No one is clearly liable.

This is the responsibility gap.

Why This Happens

Every actor has a plausible defense:

- **The Provider:** "We never claimed the answers are correct."
- **The MSP:** "We only delivered infrastructure. Verification is the customer's responsibility."
- **The Company:** "We trusted the service. We are not AI experts."
- **The Engineer:** "I used an approved tool. You cannot verify everything."

Each defense is individually understandable. Together they yield: No one is responsible.

The Structural Cause

The problem is not malicious intentions. The problem is the architecture of the contractual relationships.

Traditional IT: - System does something → Result is wrong → Bug → Manufacturer must patch - Clear causality, clear responsibility

LLM: - System does something → Result is wrong → System property → No one must patch - No clear causality, no clear responsibility

The LLM has no bug. It works as designed. It delivers stochastic outputs. That these are sometimes wrong is not a defect—it is the principle.

10.4 Responsibility Theater: Polite Language Without Liability

LLMs can formulate very politely:

"I would like to point out that..." "Please note that..." "I recommend verifying this..."

This sounds like responsibility. It is not.

What a Human Means

When a consultant says: "I recommend verifying this," it means: - They have thought about it - They have doubts - They assume partial responsibility for the recommendation - They can be sued if the recommendation was grossly wrong

What the LLM "Means"

When an LLM says: "I recommend verifying this," it means: - The training data contained such formulations - The probability for this word combination was high - There is no "thinking," no "doubt" - The system cannot be sued

The Theater

The LLM simulates responsibility. It uses the language of responsibility without the substance.

This is dangerous because: - Users interpret the polite language as competence - Disclaimers ("Please verify") are considered sufficient - The illusion of care arises where there is none

An Example

LLM answer:

"Based on my analysis of the documents, the maximum latency is 50 ms (see Document K-2024-07, page 34). I recommend comparing this value with the test protocols to ensure it applies under real conditions."

This sounds exemplary. The system recommends verification. It shows caution.

The reality:

- "Based on my analysis"—there is no analysis, only pattern matching
- "I recommend"—there is no recommendation, only probable word combination
- The disclaimer is trained behavior, not genuine caution

- The formulation was chosen because it was positively rated in training data

The engineer sees: The system is cautious. It even warns. The reality is: The system has no idea whether the warning is warranted.

The Liability Problem

- Can you blame a system for not warning—when it sometimes warns and sometimes does not?
- Can you impute negligence to a system—when it has no intent?
- Can you hold a system accountable—when it is not a legal entity?
- The answer is three times: No.

The LLM is not a legal subject. It cannot assume responsibility. Its "recommendations" are legally meaningless.

10.5 The Consequence: Liability Falls on the Weakest

When no one is clearly liable, the following happens in practice:

Step 1: The Company Bears the Damage

€180,000 in property damage. The company pays. It has no realistic way to shift the damage to provider or MSP.

Step 2: Internal Search for the Guilty

Management asks: "How could this happen? Who approved this?"

The finger points at the engineer. He approved the wrong specification.

Step 3: Disciplinary Consequences

The engineer gets a warning. Or is transferred. Or loses his job.

Not because he is legally liable. But because someone must be at fault.

Step 4: The System Remains

The LLM system stays in use. It was not recognized as defective after all. It "worked." The error lay with the user who did not verify.

The Pattern

Liability flows downward. From the provider (who protects himself contractually) to the MSP (who protects himself contractually) to the company (which bears the damage) to the engineer (who feels the consequences).

The engineer is the weakest link. He has no negotiating power. He cannot dictate liability clauses. He bears the risk.

10.6 What This Means for Practice

For Companies

1. **The contract does not protect you.** The liability exclusions protect the provider, not you.
2. **The responsibility remains internal.** Regardless of what the contract says—the damage hits you.
3. **Define processes.** Who verifies? Who approves? Who documents? These are not optional questions.

For Engineers

1. **You bear the practical risk.** Not legally (hopefully), but practically.
2. **Document everything.** Every verification, every reservation, every follow-up question.
3. **Say "No."** If time for verification is lacking, say so. In writing.

For Legislators

1. **The responsibility gap is real.** It arises not from malice but from structure.
2. **The AI Liability Directive is missing.** Without clear liability rules, the gap remains.
3. **The AI Act is not enough.** Obligations without liability are meaningless.

10.7 Key Points

- **No one is clearly liable.** Provider, MSP, company, engineer—everyone has a plausible defense.
- **The responsibility gap is structural.** Stochastic systems do not fit into liability law for deterministic products.
- **Polite language is not responsibility.** LLMs simulate care through trained phrases.
- **Liability flows downward.** In the end, the weakest link suffers the consequences—usually the engineer.
- **Contracts protect providers, not customers.** The liability exclusions are one-sided.

- **Processes and documentation are mandatory.** Not for compliance—for the protection of your own employees.
- **Legal clarification is pending.** Until then: Those who deploy AI bear the risk.

Liability is unclear. But can the risk at least be insured? Chapter 11 examines the limits of insurability of stochastic systems.

Chapter 11: Insurance of the Uninsurable?

Chapter 10 showed: Liability is unclear. No one is clearly liable. The damage stays with the company.

The obvious question: Can you insure the risk?

The answer is more complicated than hoped.

11.1 Stochastic Risks Are Hard to Insure

Insurance works on a simple principle: Many pay in, few have damages, the premiums cover the damages plus profit.

This requires: - The risk is calculable - The damage amount is estimable - The damage cases are independent of each other - There is historical data

With Traditional IT Risks

Server failure:

- Probability: statistically known (MTBF values)
- Damage amount: revenue loss per hour × expected downtime
- Independence: A server at Customer A does not affect Customer B
- Data: Decades of experience

This can be insured. And is insured.

Cyberattack:

- Probability: more difficult, but statistically recordable
- Damage amount: variable, but with upper limits
- Independence: limited (ransomware waves)
- Data: increasingly available

This can be insured—with restrictions and rising premiums.

With LLM Errors

Wrong answer leads to wrong decision:

- Probability: unknown
- Damage amount: unknown (from €0 to total loss)
- Independence: no (correlated errors through shared model)
- Data: practically none

This cannot be insured. Not yet. Perhaps never.

The Correlation Problem

With traditional risks, damage cases are largely independent. If Company A's server catches fire, this does not increase the probability that Company B's server catches fire.

With LLM errors, it is different.

Scenario: An error in the model causes all users to receive a wrong answer for a particular question.

- Company A: Error in specification
- Company B: Error in specification
- Company C: Error in specification
- ...

Thousands of damage cases simultaneously. From the same cause. This is called "cumulative risk"—every insurer's nightmare.

The insurance industry has experience with this: natural disasters, pandemics, systemic financial crises. Such risks are difficult to insure or only with very high premiums.

The Data Gap

Insurance companies need data. They must know: - How often does damage occur? - How high is the typical damage? - What factors influence the risk?

For LLM errors, this data does not exist: - The technology is too new - Damage cases are rarely classified as "LLM errors" - The dark figure is high (who admits to having trusted an AI?)

Without data, no calculation. Without calculation, no insurance—or only at prohibitive prices.

11.2 What Cyber Insurance Does Not Cover

"We have cyber insurance. That covers AI risks, right?"

No.

What Cyber Insurance Typically Covers

Risk	Covered?
Hacker attack	Yes
Ransomware	Yes (often with sublimit)
Data loss through attack	Yes
Business interruption through IT failure	Yes
Data protection violation (GDPR fines)	Partially
Forensics and recovery	Yes

What Cyber Insurance Does Not Cover

Risk	Covered?
Wrong business decision based on IT output	No
Faulty product specification through software	No
Damage through substantively wrong AI answer	No
Reputational damage through AI error	Rarely
Liability claims for faulty AI advice	No

The Crucial Difference

Cyber insurance covers **technical incidents**: Systems are attacked, fail, or are compromised.

It does not cover **substantive errors**: The system functions technically flawlessly but delivers wrong results.

An LLM that gives a wrong answer is not a cyber incident. The system was not hacked. It did not fail. It did what it was supposed to—just wrongly.

The Exclusion Clauses

Most cyber policies contain exclusions such as:

"This policy does not include damages from decisions made on the basis of IT systems."

Or:

"Damages from faulty or incomplete data, software, or algorithms, are excluded from this policy, unless caused by an insured cyber incident."

This is not a coincidence. The insurers know they cannot calculate this risk.

11.3 Product Liability Insurance and AI Outputs

"Then product liability—after all, the LLM is a product."

That is also more complicated.

What Product Liability Insurance Covers

Product liability insurance covers damages caused by defective products. "Defective" means: The product does not meet the legitimate safety expectation.

Classic example: - Company sells brake pads - Brake pads fail → Accident - Product liability: The brake pad was defective

The Problem with LLM Outputs

Is the LLM the product?

Possibly. The new Product Liability Directive (EU) 2024/2853 covers software.

But: Is a wrong answer a "defect"?

The model generated a probability distribution and sampled from it. That is not a defect—that is the principle.

The safety expectation for an LLM is unclear: - May one expect all answers to be correct? (No—every provider warns against it) - May one expect no answer to be wrong? (No—that is technically impossible) - What may one expect?

As long as that is unclear, the insurance coverage is also unclear.

The Causal Chain

Product liability requires causality: The product caused the damage.

With traditional products:

- Brake pad fails → Car does not brake → Accident
- Clear causality

With LLM:

- LLM gives answer → Engineer reads answer → Engineer decides → Decision is wrong → Product is wrongly specified → Product fails → Damage

The engineer stands in the middle. He decided to trust the answer. Did he interrupt the causal chain?

Insurers will argue: The damage was not caused by the LLM but by the engineer's decision to trust the answer.

Coverage Gaps in Practice

Even if product liability insurance theoretically applies:

Aspect	Problem
Deductible	Often €10,000–50,000—does not cover small damages
Sublimits	AI risks often limited to low amounts
Exclusions	"Advisory errors" often excluded
Premiums	For AI risks often prohibitive or not quoted

11.4 Special Insurance for AI?

The market is developing. Some insurers offer "AI Insurance" or "Algorithm Liability."

What Is Offered

Product	Coverage
AI Liability Insurance	Liability damages from AI decisions
Algorithm Error Coverage	Errors in algorithmic decisions
Technology E&O	Errors in technical services

The Restrictions

Availability: Few providers, limited capacity.

Premiums: High, often 2–5% of coverage amount per year.

Coverage amounts: Limited, typically €1–10 million.

Exclusions: Long and detailed:

- Known errors (if the model was wrong before)
- Intent (if you knew the system was unreliable)
- Regulatory fines (penalties under AI Act) - Reputational damages (often excluded)

Obligations: Strict requirements:

- Documentation of all AI decisions
- Regular audits
- Demonstrate human oversight
- Incident reporting within 24 hours

The Reality

For most mid-sized companies, these policies are: - Too expensive (premiums in the five-figure range) - Too limited (sublimits, exclusions) - Too demanding (obligations require personnel and processes)

Those who can afford this are often companies that would also have the resources for their own validation.

11.5 The Residual Risk Bearer: In the End, Always the Customer

The analysis shows a clear picture:

What Is Insurable

Risk	Insurable?
Server fails	Yes
Cyberattack	Yes
Data loss	Yes
LLM gives wrong answer	Barely
Decision based on LLM answer is wrong	No
Product defect through wrong specification	Partially

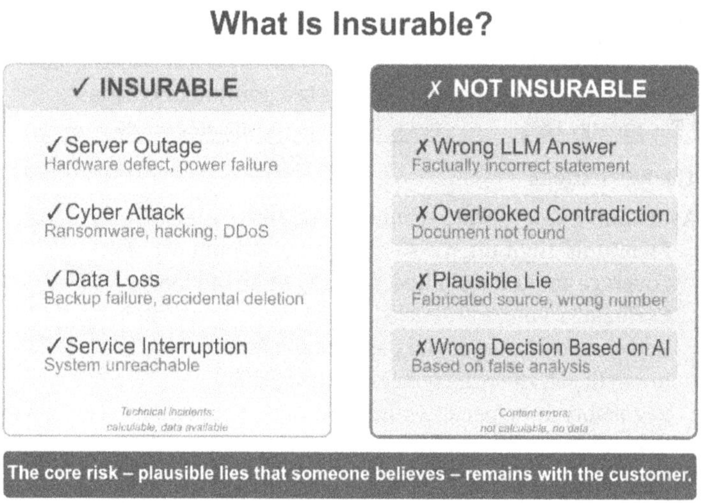

Figure 10 What is insurable and what is not: Technical infrastructure yes, content errors no. The core risk – plausible lies that someone believes – remains with the customer.

What Is Not Insurable

The core risk—that an LLM produces plausible lies and someone believes them—is not insurable.

Not because insurers are malicious. But because:

- The risk is not calculable
- The damage cases are correlated

- The data basis is missing
- The causality is unclear

The Consequence

The customer bears the residual risk.

Not the provider. Their terms of use exclude liability. Not the MSP. Their contract excludes substantive liability. Not the insurance. It does not cover the risk.

The customer.

The company that uses the service, that pays the €144,000 per year, and that hopes everything goes well.

The Irony

The promise of the managed service was: Someone else takes the responsibility.

The reality: No one takes responsibility. It stays with the customer.

The managed service does not reduce the risk. It obscures it. It does not distribute it. It concentrates it on the weakest link in the chain.

11.6 What This Means for Decisions

Before Deploying an LLM System

Questions that must be answered:

1. **What damage potential exists?**
   - Maximum single damage
   - Maximum total damage with systematic error
   - Reputational damage (not insurable)
2. **What insurance applies?**
   - Cyber policy: Check exclusions
   - Product liability: Check coverage for software
   - D&O: Covers executive fault, not operational errors
3. **What remains uninsured?**
   - Honest answer: Most of it
   - Define risk budget: How much loss is bearable?
4. **Who bears the risk internally?**
   - Management: Decision to deploy AI
   - Department: Operational use
   - Engineer: Professional responsibility

The Risk Decision

Every company that deploys an LLM for critical applications implicitly makes a risk decision:

"We accept the residual risk that the system gives wrong answers and we bear the consequences."

This decision should be made explicitly. By management. Documented with a clear view of the consequences.

Documentation as Protection

If not insurable, then at least documented:

- **Processes:** Who verifies? Who approves?
- **Decisions:** Why was the LLM trusted?
- **Reservations:** What concerns existed?
- **Escalations:** When was management informed?

Documentation does not protect against damage. But it protects against the accusation of having acted negligently.

11.7 Key Points

- **Stochastic risks are hard to insure.** Unknown probabilities, correlated damages, missing data.
- **Cyber insurance does not cover substantive errors.** It covers technical incidents, not wrong decisions.
- **Product liability applies only conditionally.** Causality is unclear when a human stands in between.
- **Special insurance exists but is expensive and limited.** Not practical for most mid-sized companies.
- **The core risk remains uninsured.** Plausible lies that someone believes—there is no policy for that.
- **The customer bears the residual risk.** Not the provider, not the MSP, not the insurance.
- **The risk decision must be explicit.** Those who deploy AI accept a residual risk. This should happen consciously.
- **Documentation is the only protection.** Not against damage—but against the accusation of negligence.

Part 3 "The Consequences" is complete. The balance is sobering: unclear liability, uninsurable risk, responsibility with the customer. Part 4 asks: What can work nonetheless? How do you deploy LLMs sensibly—with open eyes for the limits?

Part 4: What Could Work

Chapter 12: LLM as Tool, Not as Decision-Maker

Parts 1–3 analyzed the problem. The result is sobering: AI as managed service for critical applications does not work structurally. Liability is unclear. The risk is uninsurable.

Part 4 asks: What can work as an alternative?

The answer begins with a distinction: Tool or decision-maker?

12.1 The Distinction

A hammer is a tool. It does what the craftsman does. The decision lies with the human.

No one would say: "The hammer decided to drive the nail in there."

With LLMs, the boundary is less clear. The system answers in complete sentences. It formulates recommendations. It sounds like a consultant.

But it is a tool. It should be treated as a tool.

The Difference in Practice

LLM as decision-maker:

- LLM analyzes documents
- LLM identifies contradiction
- LLM result is adopted
- Engineer implements

LLM as tool:

- LLM searches documents
- LLM suggests candidates for contradictions
- Engineer verifies each candidate
- Engineer decides what is a real contradiction
- Engineer documents his decision

The difference seems subtle. It is fundamental.

In the first case, responsibility lies with the system. In the second case, it lies with the human.

In the first case, the system's error becomes the product's error. In the second case, the system's error is caught by the human—or consciously adopted.

12.2 The Researcher Model

The Researcher Model defines the role of the LLM clearly: It is a researcher, not an expert witness.

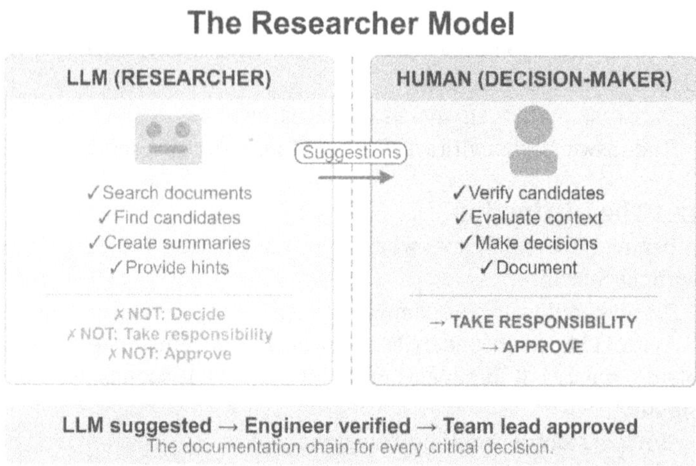

Figure 11 The Researcher Model: The LLM finds candidates. The human verifies, evaluates, decides, and takes responsibility. Clear separation of roles.

What a Researcher Does

A human researcher in a law firm: - Searches files for relevant passages - Marks potentially important sections - Summarizes documents - Creates lists of findings

A human researcher does not: - Provide legal assessment - Decide what is relevant and what is not - Sign the briefs - Appear in court

The lawyer reviews the research. He evaluates. He decides. He signs.

The LLM as Researcher

The same model works for LLMs:

The LLM does: - Search documents - Find candidates for contradictions - Create summaries - Suggest cross-references - Formulate questions that should be verified

The LLM does not: - Decide whether a contradiction is relevant - Assess whether a specification is correct - Grant approval - Assume responsibility

A Concrete Example

Query: "Find all passages where latency assumptions are made."

LLM answer (Researcher Model):

Found candidates for latency assumptions:

1. Document K-2024-07, page 34: "maximum latency 50 ms"
2. Document T-2024-03, page 12: "measured latencies up to 325 ms"
3. Document A-2023-11, page 7: "collision avoidance assumes 75 ms"
4. Document S-2024-01, page 23: "latency negligible" (no numeric value)

Note: This list may be incomplete. Please check the documents for additional passages.

What the engineer now does:

1. Verify each candidate in the original
2. Evaluate context (average? maximum? laboratory condition?)
3. Identify and document contradictions
4. Decide which contradictions are critical
5. Propose and approve measures

The LLM took work off his hands: The search through 2,000 pages. The engineer retains the responsibility: The evaluation and decision.

12.3 Why This Works

The Researcher Model solves several problems:

Problem 1: Plausible Lies

If the LLM produces a plausible lie—for example, invents a page number—this is noticed during verification. The engineer opens page 34 and sees what is actually on the page.

The lie is not adopted. It is discovered and intercepted.

Problem 2: Incompleteness

If the LLM overlooks Document C because "delay" is used instead of "latency"—the note "may be incomplete" serves as a reminder.

The engineer can search specifically: "Are there synonyms for latency that I should check?"

Problem 3: Responsibility

Responsibility is clear: The engineer decided. Not the system.

If an error occurs later, there is someone responsible. A human who made a decision. A decision that is documented.

Problem 4: Liability

The liability question becomes simpler. Not: "Did the LLM make an error?" But: "Did the engineer verify carefully?"

That is a question the legal system can answer. With known standards. With established criteria.

12.4 The Documentation Obligation

The Researcher Model works only with documentation.

What Must Be Documented

Element	Example
Query to the LLM	"Find all passages with latency assumptions"
LLM answer	List of candidates (complete)
Verification by engineer	"Candidates 1–4 verified on 15.01.2026"
Assessment	"Candidate 1 vs. Candidate 2: contradiction, critical"
Decision	"Specification will be adjusted to max. 75 ms"
Approval	"Approved by Eng. Müller, 16.01.2026"

Why Documentation Is Important

For quality: Documentation forces reflection. Anyone who writes "I have verified" must actually verify.

For traceability: Later, the process by which a decision came about can be reconstructed. What information was available? What was considered?

For liability: In case of damage, the documentation shows: Work was done carefully. There was a process. It was not negligence.

For learning: Errors can be analyzed. Where did the LLM fail? Where did verification fail? What must be improved?

The Formula

For critical applications:

LLM proposed → Engineer verified → Team lead approved

This chain must be documented. For every decision based on LLM input.

This is laborious. This is the price for safe deployment.

12.5 When the Researcher Model Is Not Enough

There are limits.

High Frequency

If thousands of decisions are made every day, not every decision can be individually verified. The Researcher Model does not scale arbitrarily.

Solution: Sampling, statistical quality control, automated plausibility checks—with the awareness that errors will slip through.

Time Pressure

If the answer is needed in seconds, no human verification is possible.

Solution: For time-critical applications, the Researcher Model is unsuitable. Either you accept the risk of error or you do without LLMs.

Lacking Expertise

If no one in the company has the competence to verify the LLM outputs, the Researcher Model does not help.

Solution: First build competence, then deploy LLM. Not the other way around.

12.6 The Cultural Change

The Researcher Model requires a cultural change.

Away from: "The AI says..."

In many companies, an attitude has crept in:

"The AI says the latency is 50 ms."

This is a shift of responsibility. The AI "says" nothing. It generates character sequences.

Toward: "The system found, I have verified..."

The new attitude:

"The system found Document K. I have verified: It says 50 ms as an average value. The maximum value in the tests is 325 ms. This is a contradiction."

This is longer. This is more laborious. This is correct.

The Leadership Task

Leaders must exemplify this cultural change:

- Do not ask: "What does the AI say?"
- But ask: "What have you verified? What conclusion have you reached?"
- Do not praise: "It's great how quickly the AI found that."
- But praise: "It's great how thoroughly you verified the AI results."
- Do not criticize: "The AI made an error."
- But analyze: "How can we detect such errors earlier in the future?"

12.7 Key Points

- **LLM is tool, not decision-maker.** The distinction is fundamental for safe deployment.
- **The Researcher Model defines clear roles.** LLM finds candidates. Human verifies, evaluates, decides.
- **Plausible lies are discovered during verification**, provided the verification actually takes place.
- **Documentation is mandatory.** "LLM proposed → Engineer verified → Team lead approved"—for every critical decision.
- **The model does not scale arbitrarily.** With high frequency or time pressure, it is not applicable.
- **Without expertise, no verification.** Those who cannot evaluate cannot verify. First competence, then LLM.
- **Cultural change is necessary.** Away from "The AI says" toward "I have verified and decided."

The Researcher Model defines the role of the LLM. But what organizational prerequisites does it require? Chapter 13 describes what must exist in the company before the first LLM service is commissioned.

Chapter 13: Organizational Prerequisites

Chapter 12 described the Researcher Model: LLM as tool, human as decision-maker.

This works only if certain prerequisites are met. This chapter describes what must exist in the company before the first LLM service is commissioned.

13.1 Internal Validation Competence Before External Service

The most important prerequisite: You must be able to verify before you buy.

The Paradox Again

Chapter 7 showed the following paradox:

Competence	Can Validate	Needs LLM
High	Yes	Less
Medium	Partially	With risk
Low	No	Not sensible at all

Those who have the competence to verify need the service less. Those who need the service cannot verify safely.

The Consequence

First competence, then service.

Before you commission an LLM service for drone specifications, you need: - Engineers who understand drone specifications - Engineers who can recognize contradictions - Engineers who have time to verify

If you do not have these engineers, the service does not help. It only creates an illusion of support.

The Sequence

Wrong:

1. Commission LLM service
2. Hope it works
3. Notice that no one can verify
4. Produce errors

Right:

1. Build internal competence
2. Define processes

3. Introduce LLM service as tool
4. Competent employees verify the results

The second variant is slower. It is also the only one that works.

13.2 Those Who Cannot Evaluate Answers Buy Blind

A sentence that is uncomfortable:

If you cannot judge whether an LLM answer is correct, you should not use the LLM for that task.

Why This Is So

An LLM can give wrong answers. We have discussed this extensively. The answers sound plausible. They can be wrong.

If no one can verify whether the answer is correct, one of two things happens:

Scenario A: The answer is adopted. Without verification. With all the risks.

Scenario B: The answer is discarded. Without verification. In that case, the LLM was useless.

In both cases, the LLM created no value. In the first case, it created risk.

The Exception

There are cases where you can use LLMs even without being competent in output verification: When the consequences of an error are bearable.

- **Brainstorming:** Wrong ideas are discarded. No damage.
- **Drafts:** Will be revised anyway. Errors are noticed.
- **Research for non-critical topics:** If it is not correct, it is not serious.

For critical applications—drone specifications, medical documentation, legal analysis—this exception does not exist.

13.3 AI Competence Under Art. 4 AI Act

The AI Act requires AI competence. This is not a recommendation—it is law.

Art. 4 AI Act: AI Competence

> *"Providers and deployers of AI systems shall take measures to ensure [...] a sufficient level of AI literacy among their staff [...]."*

The competence must be appropriate for: - The type of AI system - The context of use - The persons affected

What This Means Concretely

For a company that deploys LLMs for critical applications:

Group	Required Competence
Users (Engineers)	Understand how LLMs work; know limits; master verification methods
Managers	Understand risks; supervise processes; provide resources
IT Department	Technical aspects; data protection; integration
Compliance	Regulatory requirements; documentation obligations

The Training Obligation

Art. 4 is not optional. Companies must be able to demonstrate that they have built AI competence.

This means: - Training for all relevant employees - Documentation of training - Regular refresher courses - Proof of effectiveness

A company that uses an LLM service without having trained its employees violates the AI Act. The fines can be substantial.

13.4 FRIA: Fundamental Rights Impact Assessment

The AI Act requires a fundamental rights impact assessment for high-risk AI systems.

What Is FRIA?

FRIA (Fundamental Rights Impact Assessment) is a systematic evaluation of the effects of an AI system on the fundamental rights of affected persons.

Who Must Conduct FRIA?

According to Art. 27 AI Act: Certain deployers of high-risk AI systems, particularly: - Public bodies - Private bodies providing public services - Operators of certain critical systems

What FRIA Covers

Element	Question
Description	What is the system used for?
Affected Persons	Who is affected by the decisions?
Fundamental Rights	Which fundamental rights could be impaired?
Risks	What specific risks exist?
Measures	How are risks mitigated?
Monitoring	How are effects monitored?

Relevant for Drone Development?

If the drones are deployed for critical infrastructure, public safety, or similar areas—possibly yes.

Even if FRIA is not formally required: The systematic assessment of risks is good practice. It forces reflection before damage occurs.

13.5 The Process Landscape

Before an LLM service is introduced, processes must be defined.

Process 1: Request and Use

- Who may use the LLM?
- For which tasks?
- With which restrictions?
- How are requests documented?

Process 2: Verification and Validation

- Who verifies the LLM outputs?
- According to which criteria?
- With which documentation?
- What happens in case of doubt?

Process 3: Approval and Responsibility

- Who approves decisions based on LLM input?
- How is approval documented?
- Who bears responsibility?

Process 4: Escalation and Incident

- What happens when an error is discovered?
- How is it escalated?

- Who is informed?
- How is the error analyzed?

Process 5: Continuous Improvement

- How are errors systematically captured?
- How are processes adjusted?
- How is effectiveness measured?

The Documentation

All processes must be documented. Not for the drawer—for practice.

The documentation serves: - Training of new employees - Traceability in case of errors - Proof to auditors - Continuous improvement

13.6 Resource Planning

The Researcher Model costs time. This time must be planned.

The Calculation

Chapter 7 showed it:

Activity	Without LLM	With LLM
Search documents	2 hours	5 minutes
Verify results	–	45 minutes
Analyze contradictions	1 hour	1 hour
Check what is missing	–	1 hour
Document	30 minutes	30 minutes
Total	**3.5 hours**	**3:20 hours**

The savings are minimal. If any.

What This Means for Planning

Wrong planning: > "With the LLM, we will complete the specification review in half the time."

Correct planning: > "With the LLM, the nature of work changes. Total time remains similar. Quality can increase if we verify properly."

The Consequence for Projects

Those who introduce an LLM hoping to save personnel will be disappointed. Either:

- Verification is skipped → Quality risk
- Verification is conducted → No savings

The benefit lies elsewhere:

- Different kind of work (less searching, more evaluating)

- Possibly better results (if the LLM finds things that would otherwise be overlooked)
- Support during peak loads

But not: Less personnel for the same quality.

13.7 The Checklist Before Starting

Before an LLM service for critical applications is commissioned:

Competence

- ☐ Do we have employees who can professionally evaluate the LLM outputs?
- ☐ Are these employees trained in the use of LLMs?
- ☐ Do they understand the limits and risks?
- ☐ Do they have time for verification and documentation?

Processes

- ☐ Are potential users of the LLM defined?
- ☐ Are output verifiers defined?
- ☐ Who approves the decisions, has someone been allocated to this end?
- ☐ Is there an escalation process for errors?

Documentation

- ☐ Are requests documented?
- ☐ Are verifications documented?
- ☐ Are decisions documented?
- ☐ Is the documentation audit-proof?

Compliance

- ☐ Do we meet the AI competence requirements under Art. 4 AI Act?
- ☐ Is FRIA required? If yes: conducted?
- ☐ Are the Deployer obligations under AI Act known and implementable?

Resources

- ☐ Is time for verification and validation planned?
- ☐ Are expectations realistic (no miracle time savings)?
- ☐ Is budget available for training and processes?

Risk

- ☐ Is the residual risk accepted (management decision)?
- ☐ Is it known what is not insured?
- ☐ Is it documented who bears responsibility?

13.8 Key Points

- **First competence, then service.** Those who cannot verify buy blind.
- **Art. 4 AI Act requires AI competence.** This is law, not recommendation. Training obligation for all relevant employees.
- **FRIA may be required.** Systematic impact assessment for fundamental rights with high-risk systems.
- **Processes must be defined.** Use, verification, approval, escalation—before the system goes live.
- **Plan time for verification.** The LLM saves no time when properly verified. It changes the nature of work.
- **Take the checklist seriously.** Every unchecked item is a risk.
- **No safe deployment without preparation.** The prerequisites are not optional—they are the foundation.

The organizational prerequisites are clarified. But how do you deal with dependence on external APIs? Chapter 14 describes an alternative: Version pinning with local models.

Chapter 13a: The Offshore Parallel

13a.1 The Misunderstanding

A German company commissions an Indian team to develop a software component.

The German project manager writes: "We need a module for user management. Follow best practices."

He expects questions. Suggestions. Discussion. Perhaps even pushback if something does not seem sensible.

The Indian team delivers. On time. Exactly to specification.

Only: The specification was incomplete. Both sides knew this. The German expected the team to fill the gaps or at least address them. The team expected further instructions.

Both waited. Neither spoke.

The result works. Technically. But it does not fit.

13a.2 Hierarchy and Expectation

The conflict is not a quality problem. It is a culture problem.

In German work culture: Thinking along is expected. Those who see a problem and stay silent have failed. Initiative is mandatory.

In Indian work culture: The boss sets the direction. Those who contradict without being asked question authority. Waiting for instructions is respect.

Both attitudes are rational. Both work—in their context.

The problem arises when they meet:

German Expectation	Indian Interpretation
"Open assignment"	"Unclear leadership"
"Think along!"	"What exactly should we do?"
"Ask questions!"	"We do not disturb without reason"
"Tell us if something does not fit!"	"Criticism is not our role"

The German thinks: "They are not getting back to me—so everything is clear."

The Indian thinks: "No further instructions—so we continue as discussed."

Both are right. Both are wrong.

13a.3 The LLM Parallel

Now replace the Indian team with an LLM.

You prompt: “Analyze this document and show me the most important problems.”

You expect: The system recognizes what “important” means. It asks when context is missing. It says “I am not sure” when it is not sure.

The LLM delivers. Quickly. Plausibly formulated.

Only: It chose the definition of “important” itself. It did not address the missing contexts. It did not report uncertainty.

You waited for questions. The system waited for more precise instructions.

Neither spoke.

German Expectation of LLM	What the LLM Does
“Think along!”	Generates most probable continuation
“Ask if unclear!”	Answers anyway
“Say when you are uncertain!”	Formulates confidently
“Report problems!”	Delivers result without comment

The parallel is not perfect. An Indian team understands the assignment—it just waits for approval. An LLM does not understand—it generates.

But the effect is the same: The result does not match the expectation because the expectation was never made explicit.

13a.4 What Works

German companies that work successfully with Indian teams have learned one thing: Expectations must be explicit.

Not: “Follow best practices.”

But: “Use OAuth 2.0 for authentication. Document every endpoint. Report daily at 2:00 PM with three questions, even if you have none.”

Not: “Let us know if something does not fit.”

But: “Before every implementation, you send a draft. Without approval, no coding.”

Not: “Think along.”

But: Defined checkpoints. Structured reviews. Mandatory questions.

The collaboration works—but it requires work on the German side. The expectation that the counterpart “will know what is meant” must die.

13a.5 Transfer to LLM Projects

The same principles apply to LLMs:

Instead of open prompts: Structured instructions

Not: "Summarize the document."

But: "List the five most important technical requirements. For each requirement: page number, verbatim quote, possible conflict with other requirements."

Instead of expected questions: Built-in checkpoints

Not: "Analyze and report problems."

But: "Analyze Section 3. Stop after each subsection. List uncertainties explicitly before continuing."

Instead of implicit thinking along: Explicit validation loops

Not: "The LLM will notice when something is wrong."

But: Human verifies every output. Defined criteria. Documented decision.

13a.6 The Uncomfortable Realization

Those who failed with Indian teams and blamed "the Indians" will also fail with LLMs.

Those who learned that successful collaboration requires explicit structures—regardless of whether the counterpart comes from Mumbai or from a data center—have an advantage.

The work does not lie with the counterpart. It lies with the one who gives the assignment.

This is uncomfortable. But it is the truth.

13a.7 Key Points

- German work culture expects implicit thinking along—Indian work culture expects explicit instructions
- LLMs behave similarly: They do not ask, do not report uncertainty, deliver anyway
- Successful offshore collaboration requires explicit structures, not cultural adaptation
- The same principles apply to LLM projects: Structured prompts, built-in checkpoints, defined validation

- The responsibility for clear assignments lies with the client—not with the executor

Status: January 2026 Classification: Part 4—What Could Work, between Chapters 13 and 14

Chapter 14: Version Pinning Instead of API Dependency

One problem we have not yet addressed: What happens when the model changes?

With cloud APIs, this is the rule. The model is updated. Without warning. Without consultation. The behavior changes. Your tests are worthless.

There is an alternative.

14.1 The Problem of API Dependency

The Promise

Cloud APIs promise: - Always the latest model - Automatic improvements - No maintenance needed - Scalability on demand

The Reality

Cloud APIs mean: - The model changes without control - "Improvements" can be deteriorations (for your use case) - No replicability - Dependency on the provider

A Concrete Example

January 2026: You have carefully developed your prompts. The system reliably finds latency specifications in your documents. The hit rate is good. You trust the system.

February 2026: The provider updates the model. "Improved reasoning capabilities," says the changelog.

Suddenly: - Some prompts no longer work as expected - The answers are more detailed but less accurate - The source citations have a different format - Your downstream processes break

You changed nothing. Yet nothing works anymore.

The Consequence for Critical Applications

For non-critical applications, this is annoying. For critical applications, it is dangerous.

If you use an LLM for specification review, you need: - replicable results - Predictable behavior - Controlled changes - Time for regression tests

Cloud APIs do not offer this.

14.2 Version Pinning: The Principle

Version pinning means: You fix the model version. The model does not change until you actively switch.

How This Works

Option A: Local Model - You operate the model yourself (see Chapter 3) - You decide when to update - Full control, full responsibility

Option B: Versioned API - Some providers offer versioned endpoints - You explicitly call Version X - The version remains stable (for a defined period)

Option C: Snapshot Service - Specialized providers offer "frozen" models - Guaranteed stability for defined periods - Higher costs, more control

The Trade-off

Aspect	Version Pinning	Current API
Control	High	Low
Replicability	Yes	No
Latest features	No	Yes
Maintenance effort	High	Low
Costs (local)	High (infrastructure)	Low (pay-per-use)
Dependency	Low	High

14.3 Local Model: The Sovereign Option

For maximum control: A local, frozen model.

The Advantages

Replicability: The same input yields (with the same configuration) the same output. Always. This enables: - Regression tests - Error analysis - Audit evidence

Independence: No provider can: - Change the model - Discontinue the service - Raise prices - See your data

Predictability: You decide: - When you update - How much time you plan for tests - Whether you update at all

The Costs

Chapters 2.3 and Appendix F have shown it: - Infrastructure: €120,000–500,000 initial - Operations: €100,000–150,000 per year - Personnel: Specialized expertise needed

This is substantial. But it is predictable. And it is independent.

When It Is Worth It

Local models are worth it when: - The application is critical (error = damage) - The data is confidential (no cloud upload possible) - Replicability is important (regulated industries) - Usage is intensive (>8,000 GPU hours/month)

14.4 The Testing Effort for Version Changes

Whether local or API—eventually you will want to change the version. Then the work begins.

What Must Be Tested

Functional Tests:

- Does the new model deliver the same results?
- Are the answers better, the same, or worse?
- Do all prompts still work?

Regression Tests:

- Run known test cases
- Document deviations
- Analyze critical deviations

Integration Tests:

- Do downstream processes still work?
- Do systems still parse the answers correctly?
- Are the formats compatible?

The Testing Effort in Practice

For a critical system, plan for:

Test Phase	Effort
Update test cases	2–5 days
Run regression tests	3–10 days
Analyze deviations	2–5 days
Adapt prompts	1–5 days
Integration tests	2–5 days
Documentation	1–2 days
Total	**11–32 days**

This is substantial. That is why you do not make changes lightly.

The Consequence

Fewer Updates = More Control

A company that works carefully changes the model version: - Not with every provider update - Not spontaneously - But with thorough planning, testing, and documentation

This means: You are not on the cutting edge. The new model may be better. But you know your model works.

14.5 Less Capable, but Predictable

There is an objection:

“Local models are smaller and less capable than the large cloud models.”

This is true. And it may not matter.

The Capability Question

Model	Parameters	Performance	Operation
GPT-4 (Cloud)	~1,800B (estimated)	Excellent	API only
Claude 3 (Cloud)	Unknown	Excellent	API only
Llama 3.1 405B	405B	Very good	Local possible (demanding)
Llama 3.1 70B	70B	Good	Local feasible
Mistral Large	123B	Good	Local feasible

What “Good Enough” Means

For many tasks, “good” is sufficient: - Searching documents: 70B is enough - Creating summaries: 70B is enough - Finding candidates: 70B is enough

The Researcher Model (Chapter 12) does not require peak performance. It requires: - Reliability - Replicability - Control

A smaller, local model can deliver this better than a larger cloud model that can change at any time.

The Pragmatism

The question is not: “Which model is the best?”

The question is: “Which model can we operate safely?”

Sometimes the answer is: A smaller, controlled model—instead of the large, uncontrollable one.

14.6 Hybrid Approaches

It does not have to be all-or-nothing.

Approach 1: Local for Critical, Cloud for Non-Critical

- Specification review: Local model (control important)
- Marketing texts: Cloud API (errors non-critical)
- Brainstorming: Cloud API (control unimportant)

Approach 2: Local for Production, Cloud for Development

- Developing new prompts: Cloud API (fast, flexible)
- Production: Local model (stable, tested)
- Transition: Careful migration and tests

Approach 3: Versioned API with Local Fallback

- Primary: Versioned cloud API (if available)
- Fallback: Local model (if API unavailable or changed)
- Regular reconciliation between both

The Decision Matrix

Criterion	Local	Versioned API	Current API
Critical application	✓	✓	✗
Confidential data	✓	Partially	✗
Regulated industry	✓	✓	✗
Limited budget	✗	✓	✓
Limited expertise	✗	✓	✓
Maximum performance needed	✗	✗	✓

14.7 Key Points

- **Cloud APIs change without control.** Today's model is not tomorrow's model.
- **Version pinning restores control.** Fixed version = replicable results.
- **Local models are the most sovereign option.** Full control, but high costs and effort.
- **Version changes require tests.** 11–32 days of effort for a careful change.
- **Less capable can be better.** A controlled 70B model can be safer than an uncontrolled 1,800B model.

- **Hybrid approaches are possible.** Local for critical, cloud for non-critical.
- **The question is not performance, but control.** Which model can you operate safely?

Version pinning solves the stability problem. But what goes in the contract if you do use a service? Chapter 15 shows what can sensibly be agreed in SLAs—and what cannot.

Chapter 15: SLA for the Periphery

Chapter 5 showed: An SLA that guarantees correctness is impossible.

But that does not mean SLAs are useless. It means expectations must be calibrated. This chapter shows what can sensibly be agreed—and what cannot.

15.1 What Is Measurable: Availability, Response Time, Data Protection

Let us begin with what works.

Availability

Measurable: Yes. Uptime monitoring is established technology.

Sensible agreement:

Parameter	Target Value	Measurement	Consequence
System availability	99.5%	Monitoring	Service credit 10%/month
API availability	99.9%	Health checks	Service credit 5%/month
Planned maintenance	Max. 4h/month	Announcement 7 days	No charge
Max. downtime	4h continuous	Incident tickets	Special termination possible

Response Time (Technical)

Measurable: Yes. Latency can be measured.

Sensible agreement:

Parameter	Target Value	Measurement
API latency (P50)	< 1 second	Server logs
API latency (P95)	< 3 seconds	Server logs
API latency (P99)	< 10 seconds	Server logs

Support Response Time

Measurable: Yes. Ticket times can be tracked.

Sensible agreement:

Priority	Response Time	Resolution Time
Critical (system down)	30 minutes	4 hours
High (function impaired)	2 hours	8 hours
Normal (question, request)	8 hours	3 business days
Low (wish, suggestion)	2 business days	By arrangement

Data Protection

Measurable: Partially. Compliance can be audited.

Sensible agreement:

Parameter	Commitment
Data location	EU (name specific countries)
Subcontractors	List of approved subcontractors
US jurisdiction	No US companies in the chain (if possible)
Deletion	Upon request within 30 days
Audit right	Annual audit possible

15.2 What Is Not Measurable: Correctness

Now what does not work.

Attempts That Fail

Attempt 1: "95% correct answers"
Problem: Who defines "correct"? Who measures? When?
Attempt 2: "Answers are based on provided documents"
Problem: What does "based on" mean? How is this verified?
Attempt 3: "Best effort to avoid false statements"
Problem: "Best effort" is not a guarantee. It is the absence of a guarantee.

Why This Is So

Correctness with LLMs is:

- Subjective (What is "correct" for a summary?)
- Context-dependent (Correct for which purpose?)
- Non-deterministic (Same question, different answer)
- Not measurable without domain expertise

An SLA requires objective, measurable criteria. Correctness meets none of them.

The Honest Formulation

What should be in the SLA—clear and unambiguous:

Exclusion of Substantive Warranty

The provider does not warrant the substantive correctness, completeness, or suitability of the outputs generated by the system. The system produces stochastic outputs based on statistical patterns. The customer is responsible for verifying and validating all outputs before use.

This is not pretty. It is honest.

15.3 Clear Responsibility Boundaries

A good contract defines who is responsible for what.

Provider Responsibility

Area	Responsibility
Infrastructure	Operation, availability, maintenance
Security	Access control, encryption, patch management
Support	Response times, escalation, problem resolution
Compliance	GDPR, technical standards
Documentation	Technical documentation of the system

Customer Responsibility

Area	Responsibility
Content	Quality and legality of ingested documents
Validation	Verification of all outputs before use
Processes	Definition and compliance with internal verification processes
Competence	AI competence of employees (Art. 4 AI Act)
Decision	All decisions based on system outputs

The Gray Zone

There are areas that must be negotiated:

Area	Clarification Needed
Prompt optimization	Who is responsible for effective prompts?
Model selection	Who decides which model is deployed?
Updates	How are model updates communicated and tested?
Monitoring	Who monitors the quality of outputs?
Incident definition	What is an "incident" for substantive errors?

These points should be clarified before contract signing. Not after.

15.4 Sample Formulations

Here are formulations that could appear in an honest LLM service contract.

Service Description

Subject of Service

The provider makes a system for AI-assisted document analysis available to the customer. The system enables searching documents, creating summaries, and identifying potential connections.

The system is based on Large Language Models (LLMs) that produce stochastic outputs. The system's outputs are to be understood as suggestions that require professional verification by the customer.

Warranty

The provider warrants:

- The technical availability of the system according to the agreed SLAs - Compliance with the agreed data protection standards
- Provision of support according to the agreed response times

The provider does not warrant:

- The substantive correctness of system outputs
- The completeness of search results
- The suitability of outputs for specific purposes
- Freedom from errors, omissions, or inaccuracies

Cooperation Obligations

Customer Cooperation Obligations

The customer commits to:

- Having all system outputs verified by qualified personnel before use
- Establishing and documenting processes for validation and approval of system outputs
- Ensuring the AI competence of its employees according to Art. 4 AI Act
- Informing the provider immediately about systematic errors

Liability

The provider is liable without limitation for damages arising from injury to life, body, or health and for damages caused intentionally or through gross negligence.

For damages resulting from the use of system outputs, the provider is liable only in cases of intent or gross negligence and only up to the amount of compensation paid by the customer in the relevant contract year.

The provider is not liable for damages arising because the customer used system outputs without adequate verification.

Versioning

Model Versions

The provider informs the customer at least 30 days before a planned change of model version. The customer has the right to use the existing version for an additional 90 days to conduct their own tests.

In case of unplanned changes to the model version by the upstream provider, the provider informs the customer immediately and provides, where possible, the previous version for a transition period.

15.5 What Should Not Be in the Contract

Some formulations are warning signs:

Red Flags

Formulation	Problem
"AI-powered quality assurance"	Implies guarantee that does not exist
"Reliable answers"	Not defined, not measurable
"Minimized hallucinations"	Suggests solvable problem
"Intelligent document analysis"	Marketing, not service description
"Replaces manual review"	Dangerously wrong

What Should Be There Instead

Marketing Speak	Honest Formulation
"Reliable answers"	"Suggestions for professional verification"
"Intelligent analysis"	"Statistical pattern recognition"
"AI quality assurance"	"Tool to support quality assurance"
"Replaces manual review"	"Supplements manual review"

15.6 The Negotiating Position

As Customer

You have negotiating power. Use it:

1. **Demand clear exclusions.** Better to know what the provider is not liable for than to be surprised later.
2. **Require version control.** At minimum, advance notice of model changes.
3. **Insist on audit rights.** For data protection and security.
4. **Clarify US jurisdiction.** Where is your data? Who can access it?
5. **Define exit scenarios.** What happens at contract end? How do you get your data back?

As Provider

Honesty protects in the long run:

1. **Make no false promises.** The first damage case ruins reputation.
2. **Define clear boundaries.** Better to lose an order than to have to win a lawsuit.

3. **Document the disclosure.** Prove that the customer knew the risks.
4. **Offer training.** Competent customers have fewer damages.

15.7 Key Points

- Availability, response time, data protection are measurable. These points belong in the SLA.
- Correctness is not measurable. Attempts to guarantee it fail or are meaningless.
- The honest exclusion is better than the false commitment. Clear words: "We do not warrant..."
- Responsibility boundaries must be defined. Who does what? Who is liable for what?
- Version control belongs in the contract. Advance notice, transition period, testing opportunity.
- Marketing speak is a warning sign. "Intelligent," "reliable," "minimized"—ask what that concretely means.
- Negotiation before the damage is easier than after. Invest time in the contract.

The contract is clarified. But how do you make the fundamental decision whether to deploy LLMs at all? Chapter 16 provides guidance for decision-makers.

Chapter 16: Guidance for Decision-Makers

This book has analyzed much. Criticized much. Warned much.

This final chapter distills the findings into practical guidance for those who must make decisions: Should we deploy AI? How? Under what conditions?

16.1 Questions That Must Be Answered Before Implementation

Before you commission an LLM service or build a local system, these questions must be answered. Honestly.

Question 1: What Exactly Should the System Do?

Not: "Improve our processes with AI." But: "Check specification documents for contradictions in latency values."

The more concrete the task, the better you can: - Evaluate whether an LLM is suitable for it - Measure whether it works - Recognize when it does not work

Question 2: What Happens If the System Is Wrong?

Play through the failure case: - The LLM overlooks a contradiction. What then? - The LLM invents a contradiction. What then? - The LLM cites a source that does not exist. What then?

If the answer is: "That would be bad"—then you need robust verification processes. If the answer is: "That would be acceptable"—then you can be more relaxed.

Question 3: Who Can Evaluate the Outputs?

Name names. Concretely.

- Who in the company can judge whether an LLM output about drone specification is correct?
- How much time does this person have?
- What happens if this person is sick or resigns?

If you cannot name names, you have a problem.

Question 4: How Much Verification Effort Is Realistic?

Be honest:

- Will your engineers really verify every LLM output?
- Or will they start adopting results after a week?
- How do you prevent the gradual erosion of diligence?

The time pressure is real. The temptation to "trust the AI" is real. Plan for it.

Question 5: What Is Plan B?

If the service fails, is terminated, or proves unusable: - How do you continue? - Is there a process without LLM? - How long does the transition take?

Dependency on a single service is a risk. Do you have an exit strategy?

16.2 Red Flags in Provider Promises

Some formulations should make you alert.

Red Flag 1: "Replaces Manual Review"

What it means: The provider wants you to trust the system.
The reality: No serious application of an LLM for critical tasks foregoes human review.
Ask: "How exactly do you guarantee correctness? Do you assume liability?"

Red Flag 2: "Hallucinations Minimized" / "Almost No Errors"

What it means: The provider knows the problem but wants to downplay it.
The reality: "Minimized" is not a measurable standard. "Almost none" is not a guarantee.
Ask: "How do you measure this? What error rate does the system have concretely? For which tasks?"

Red Flag 3: "AI-Powered Quality Assurance"

What it means: Marketing speak for "an LLM looks it over."
The reality: Quality assurance requires validation. An LLM cannot validate (Chapter 7).
Ask: "What exactly does the system do? How is the quality of the quality assurance ensured?"

Red Flag 4: "Based on Your Documents" (as Quality Feature)

What it means: RAG (Retrieval-Augmented Generation) is used.
The reality: RAG improves relevance, not reliability. The system can still draw wrong conclusions or overlook documents.
Ask: "What happens if the system does not find a relevant document? How would we notice?"

Red Flag 5: "Industry-Leading AI Technology"

What it means: The provider uses a standard model (GPT, Claude, Llama) and sells it as their own achievement.
The reality: The model has the same limitations as with any other provider.
Ask: "Which base model do you use? What exactly is your own contribution?"

Red Flag 6: No Clear Liability Exclusions

What it means: Either the provider does not understand their own product, or they are hiding something.
The reality: Every serious provider explicitly excludes substantive liability.
Ask: "Where exactly in the contract does it say you are not liable for substantive correctness?"

16.3 The Honest Conversation with Your Own Engineer

Before you decide, have this conversation.

The Questions

To the engineer:

1. "If you had a system that gives correct outputs 80% of the time and wrong ones 20%—would you use it?"
2. "How would you recognize which output belong to the 20%?"
3. "How much time would verification cost?"
4. "What would happen if you adopted a wrong output or suggestion?"
5. "Honestly: Would you still verify every output as carefully after six months as you did so on the first day?"

What You Want to Hear

- Realistic assessment of verification possibilities
- Awareness of the limits of their own time budget

- Skepticism that does not turn into rejection
- Pragmatism without naivety

What You Do Not Want to Hear

- "Sure, this makes my work much easier."
- "If the AI says so, it's probably right."
- "Finally, I don't have to verify everything by myself anymore."

These answers show that the engineer wants to delegate responsibility to the system. This is dangerous.

16.4 "Can We Do It Without AI?"

An uncomfortable question that is asked too rarely.

The FOMO Effect

Many AI projects arise from fear: - "The competition is doing it too." - "We need to be innovative." - "The board expects AI initiatives."
These are bad reasons for technical decisions.

The Right Question

Not: "How can we deploy AI?" But: "What problem do we want to solve?" And then: "Is AI the best solution for this problem?"

Examining Alternatives

For the drone scenario—finding contradictions in 2,000 pages:

Solution	Pros and Cons
More engineers	Expensive, but reliable
Better documentation	Prevents contradictions from the start
Structured reviews	Established, verifiable
Specialized software	Deterministic, but limited
LLM support	Flexible, but unreliable

Sometimes "more staff" or "better processes" is the better answer than "AI."

The Innovation Myth

Deploying AI is not automatically innovative. It is a tool choice.

Innovative would be: - A process that prevents contradictions from arising in the first place - A documentation structure that is automatically checkable for consistency - A team structure that enables cross-functional review

Sometimes the bravest decision is: "We don't need this."

16.5 Checklist for AI Projects

A summary in checklist form.

Before the Decision

- ☐ The problem is concretely defined
- ☐ Alternatives (without AI) have been seriously examined
- ☐ The failure case scenario has been played through
- ☐ The consequences of an error are known and acceptable
- ☐ There are named individuals who can evaluate outputs

Before Commissioning

- ☐ Provider promises have been critically questioned
- ☐ The contract contains clear liability exclusions (that have been understood)
- ☐ Version control is regulated
- ☐ Data protection and US jurisdiction are clarified
- ☐ Exit strategy exists

Before Go-Live

- ☐ Internal validation competence is present
- ☐ Processes for verification and approval are defined
- ☐ Training has been conducted (Art. 4 AI Act)
- ☐ Documentation is prepared
- ☐ Resources for verification are planned (realistically)

In Operation

- ☐ Every critical decision is documented
- ☐ Errors are systematically captured
- ☐ Regular reviews of process compliance take place
- ☐ Gradual erosion of verification diligence is monitored
- ☐ Management receives honest reports

16.6 A Final Word

This book is not a plea against AI. It is a plea for honesty.

LLMs are impressive tools. They can help with research. They can generate ideas. They can create drafts.

What they cannot do: - Give guaranteed correct answers - Assume responsibility - Replace professional validation - Replace human judgment

Those who accept this can deploy LLMs sensibly.

Those who ignore this will sooner or later pay the price.

The Core Message

An LLM is a tool, not a decision-maker.
It finds candidates. The human verifies. It makes suggestions. The human decides. It supports. The human is responsible.

Those who confuse these roles have not understood the Little Helper Paradox.

16.7 Key Points

- **Be concrete.** "Introduce AI" is not a goal. "Find latency contradictions" is a goal.
- **Play through the failure case.** What happens if the system is wrong?
- **Name names.** Who can verify? Concretely, with time budget.
- **Take red flags seriously.** Marketing speak is a warning sign.
- **Talk to engineers.** Honestly, without euphemism.
- **Examine alternatives.** "Do we need AI?" is a legitimate question.
- **Use the checklist.** Before the decision, before commissioning, before go-live, in operation.
- **Honesty as principle.** Toward yourself, toward employees, toward customers.

Part 4 is complete. The book has shown: AI as managed service for critical applications does not work structurally. What can work: AI as tool, with human validation, clear processes, and honest expectations. The Little Helper Paradox is not an argument against AI. It is an argument for realism.

Conclusion: Resolving the Paradox

This book has analyzed much. It is time for a balance sheet.

What We Have Shown

Part 1: The Promise

AI as a managed service promises much: intelligent document analysis, automatic contradiction detection, and AI-powered quality assurance. The promise is attractive because in-house operations are expensive. €650,000 in the first year, €550,000 in subsequent years—just for a single LLM system with adequate competence, infrastructure, and compliance.

The temptation is understandable: Someone else should bear the costs, bring the competence, assume the responsibility.

Part 2: The Falsification

The promise does not hold. The method was simple: Try to write the contract.

SLA for availability: Works. Measurable, definable, enforceable.

SLA for correctness: Does not work. Not measurable, not definable, not enforceable.

The reason is architectural: LLMs produce stochastic outputs. They guess—highly intelligently, but they guess. The most probable answer is not the correct answer. Wrong answers are not a bug. They are a feature.

Validation fails due to the competence paradox: Those who can verify need the system less. Those who need it cannot verify.

Part 3: The Consequences

The legal situation is unclear. Civil law does not fit stochastic systems. The AI Act defines obligations but no liability. The AI Liability Directive was withdrawn. The Product Liability Directive covers software, but is a wrong answer a "defect"?

Add to this the CLOUD Act: Those who process data at US providers are subject to US jurisdiction—even with servers in Frankfurt.

The liability chain leads to nowhere. Provider, MSP, company, engineer—everyone has a plausible defense. In the end, the weakest bears the consequences.

The risk is not insurable. Stochastic errors, correlated damages, missing data—the insurance industry cannot calculate this.

Part 4: What Could Work

The alternative is not abstaining from using AI. The alternative is honesty.

The Researcher Model: LLM as tool, not as decision-maker. It finds candidates. The human verifies, evaluates, decides, is responsible.

Organizational prerequisites: First competence, then service. Those who cannot verify buy blind.

Version pinning: Control instead of dependency. A frozen model is less capable but predictable.

SLA for the periphery: Availability, response time, data protection—measurable and agreeable. Correctness—not absolute, but honestly excluded.

The Core Message in Three Sentences

1. LLMs cannot guarantee that their answers are correct. This is not a deficiency—this is the architecture.
2. What cannot be guaranteed cannot be sold as a managed service. At least not for critical applications.
3. Responsibility stays with the human. The system supports. The human decides. This cannot be delegated.

The Paradox Resolved

The Little Helper Paradox is not an argument against LLMs. It is an argument against misplaced trust.

The paradox arises when you believe: - The system replaces human verification - More help means less work - Responsibility can be delegated

The paradox resolves when you understand: - The system supplements human verification - Different help means different work - Responsibility cannot be delegated

An LLM is like a brilliant intern: fast, well-read, articulate—but without judgment. You give them tasks. You verify their results. You do not blindly sign what they present.

Those who understand this can use LLMs sensibly.

Those who ignore this will sooner or later pay the price.

Outlook

What Will Change

The technology will improve. New models will make fewer errors. But they will not stop making errors. Stochastics remains stochastics.

The legal situation will become clearer. Eventually there will be liability regulation. Courts will create precedents. The gaps will close—but slowly.

The insurance industry will develop products. When enough damage data is available, risks will become calculable. This takes years.

The first major damage will come. Somewhere an LLM will make a critical error that is not recognized in time. The consequences will make headlines. After that, the discussion will be conducted differently.

What Will Not Change

The architecture. LLMs remain stochastic. They will guess better. They will not stop guessing.

The paradox. The more a system helps, the more you trust it. The more you trust, the less you verify. This is human. This remains.

The responsibility. In the end, there is a human who decides. In the end, there is a human who is liable. Neither technology nor contracts change this.

A Final Thought

This book was created with the help of an LLM. Claude from Anthropic was researcher, sparring partner, formulation helper.

I verified every statement. I drew every conclusion myself. The errors that remain are mine.

This is exactly the division of labor this book recommends.

And perhaps this is the best summary:

Use the tool. Do not trust it blindly. Verify. Decide. Take responsibility.

This applies to LLMs. This applies to this book. This applies to everything that matters.

Stuttgart, January 2026
Michael Schmid

List of Figures

Glossary

A

AI Act Regulation (EU) 2024/1689 on Artificial Intelligence. In force since August 1, 2024. Regulates the development, placing on the market, and use of AI systems in the EU. Distinguishes risk categories from "unacceptable" to "minimal."
API (Application Programming Interface) Programming interface. Enables communication between software systems. For LLMs: The technical access point to the model through which queries are sent and responses received.

B

BGB (Bürgerliches Gesetzbuch) German Civil Code. §§ 327–327u regulate contracts for digital products since January 2022.

C

CAPEX (Capital Expenditure) One-time costs for the acquisition of hardware, software, or infrastructure. Opposite: OPEX.
Checkpoint (in GPU training) Regularly saved intermediate state of a training run. Enables resumption after interruption without a complete restart.
CLOUD Act (Clarifying Lawful Overseas Use of Data Act) US law from 2018. Allows US authorities to request data from US companies—regardless of where the data is stored.
Compliance Adherence to legal and regulatory requirements.

D

Deployer Under the AI Act: The entity that uses an AI system (as opposed to the provider, who develops it). Has specific obligations under Art. 26 AI Act.
Deterministic Predictable. A deterministic system produces the same output for the same input every time. Opposite: stochastic.

F

Fine-Tuning Further training of a pre-trained model on specific data. Adapts the model to a domain without training it from scratch.
FRIA (Fundamental Rights Impact Assessment) Required under Art. 27 AI Act for certain deployers of high-risk AI systems.

G

Gag Order Court order prohibiting disclosure of a matter. In the CLOUD Act context: US providers may not inform customers that their data has been requested.
GDPR (General Data Protection Regulation) Regulation (EU) 2016/679. Regulates the protection of personal data in the EU.
GPAI (General Purpose AI) General-purpose AI. Models such as GPT, Claude, or Llama that can be used for many different tasks. Subject to specific rules under the AI Act since August 2025.
GPU (Graphics Processing Unit) Originally developed for image processing, now central to AI training and inference due to high parallel processing capability.

H

Hallucination A widespread but misleading term for incorrect LLM outputs. Suggests malfunction, although it is normal system behavior. This book prefers "plausible lie" or "fact-free response."
HGX NVIDIA platform for high-end AI servers. 4–8 GPUs with NVLink/NVSwitch for maximum communication bandwidth. Optimized for training, not for high availability.
High-Risk AI System Category under the AI Act (Annex III). Includes AI in critical areas such as medical devices, safety components, and critical infrastructure. Subject to strict obligations.

I

Inference Running a trained model to generate outputs. Opposite: Training.
ISO 42001 International standard for AI management systems. Defines process requirements, not output quality.
ISO 27001 International standard for information security management systems.
ITAR (International Traffic in Arms Regulations) US export control regulations for defense articles.

L

Latency Delay time. In drone communication: The time between sending and receiving a message. Critical for real-time applications.
Little Helper Paradox Central concept of this book: The more you trust an LLM, the less you verify. The less you verify, the more dangerous the

trust becomes. The system that is supposed to help undermines the ability to evaluate its help.

LLM (Large Language Model) Neural network trained on large text corpora that can process and generate language. Examples: GPT, Claude, Llama, Mistral.

M

Managed Service IT service where an external provider takes over operations. Typically with SLAs for availability, support, and response times.

MSP (Managed Service Provider) Provider of managed services.

MTBF (Mean Time Between Failures) Average time between failures. A measure of hardware reliability.

N

Next-Token Prediction Fundamental principle of LLMs: The model predicts the most probable next word (token) based on the preceding context. Explains why LLMs sound plausible without "knowing."

NVLink / NVSwitch NVIDIA technologies for fast GPU-to-GPU communication in HGX systems.

O

OPEX (Operational Expenditure) Ongoing costs for operations, maintenance, and personnel. Opposite: CAPEX.

P

Parameter In neural networks: The trained weights. "70B model" = 70 billion parameters. More parameters generally means higher capability but also higher resource requirements.

PLD (Product Liability Directive) Directive (EU) 2024/2853. Explicitly covers software for the first time. Applies from December 9, 2026.

Plausible Lie Preferred term in this book for incorrect LLM outputs. Emphasizes: The answer sounds convincing but is factually wrong. Not a malfunction, but a system characteristic.

Prompt Input to an LLM. The formulation of the prompt significantly influences the quality of the response.

Provider Under the AI Act: The entity that develops or commissions the development of an AI system and places it on the market under its own name.

R

RAG (Retrieval-Augmented Generation) Architecture where an LLM receives relevant documents as context before responding. Improves relevance but does not solve the reliability problem.

Researcher Model Approach recommended in this book: LLM as researcher (finds candidates), human as decision-maker (verifies and takes responsibility).

Responsibility Theater In this book: The phenomenon where LLMs simulate responsibility awareness through polite language ("I recommend verifying...") without being able to actually assume responsibility.

Retrieval Fetching relevant documents from a database. The first step in RAG.

RLHF (Reinforcement Learning from Human Feedback) Training method that uses human feedback to improve LLM responses. Can lead models to prefer answering (incorrectly) over saying "I don't know."

S

SAN (Storage Area Network) Centralized, often redundant storage for multiple servers.

Schrems I / Schrems II CJEU rulings (2015/2020) that invalidated EU-US data transfer agreements (Safe Harbor and Privacy Shield, respectively). Named after plaintiff Max Schrems.

SLA (Service Level Agreement) Agreement on service quality. Defines measurable targets (availability, response time) and consequences for non-compliance.

Stochastic Random-based. A stochastic system can produce different outputs for the same input. LLMs are stochastic. Opposite: deterministic.

Sublimit Cap within insurance policies. Limits coverage for specific types of damage to an amount below the total coverage sum.

T

TCO (Total Cost of Ownership) Total operating costs. CAPEX plus OPEX over a defined period.

Temperature Parameter in LLM inference. Higher temperature = more variation in responses. Lower temperature = more predictable responses. Does not change the fundamental stochastic nature.

Token Smallest processing unit of an LLM. Corresponds roughly to a word or word part.

V

Validation Verification of content correctness. For LLM outputs: Requires domain expertise that the LLM itself cannot provide.

Version Pinning Fixing a model version to ensure reproducibility and control. Opposite: Using a changing cloud API.

VRAM (Video RAM) Memory on a GPU. Limits the size of models that can be loaded.

W

Contradiction Detection In the drone example: Finding inconsistent specifications in documentation (e.g., different latency values).

This glossary does not claim to be exhaustive. The definitions are tailored to the context of this book.

Bibliography

As of: January 2026

1. Textbooks and Foundational Works

AI / Machine Learning

[Ertel 2025]

Ertel, Wolfgang: *Grundkurs Künstliche Intelligenz. Eine praxisorientierte Einführung.* 6th Edition. Springer Vieweg, Wiesbaden 2025. ISBN 978-3-658-44955-1 → German-language standard textbook, all AI subdisciplines, new chapter on LLMs

[Russell/Norvig 2020]

Russell, Stuart; Norvig, Peter: *Artificial Intelligence: A Modern Approach.* 4th Edition. Pearson, 2020. ISBN 978-0-13-461099-3 → The global reference work, used at over 1,500 universities

[Burkov 2019]

Burkov, Andriy: *The Hundred-Page Machine Learning Book.* Self-published, 2019. ISBN 978-1-9995795-0-0 → Compact introduction, also available in German

[Weizenbaum 1976]

Weizenbaum, Joseph: *Computer Power and Human Reason: From Judgment to Calculation.* W. H. Freeman, 1976. ISBN 978-0-7167-0463-8 German edition: *Die Macht der Computer und die Ohnmacht der Vernunft.* Suhrkamp, 1978. → ELIZA effect, critique of AI euphoria—more relevant than ever

Managed Services

[Schmid 2026]

Schmid, Michael: *Managed Services richtig verstehen* (Understanding Managed Services). 1st Edition. it-dialog e.K., Stuttgart 2026. ISBN 978-3-96459-025-1 (Print), 978-3-96459-026-8 (E-Book) → Foundation for Chapters 1–3, definition of managed service

2. Legal Sources

EU Regulations and Directives

[AI Act 2024]

Regulation (EU) 2024/1689 of the European Parliament and of the Council of 13 June 2024 laying down harmonised rules on artificial intelligence (Artificial Intelligence Act). OJ L 2024/1689. In force since: August 1, 2024. → Risk categories, provider/deployer obligations, timeline

[Product Liability Directive 2024]

Directive (EU) 2024/2853 of the European Parliament and of the Council of 23 October 2024 on liability for defective products. OJ L 2024/2853. Applicable from: December 9, 2026. → Software as product, strict liability [AI Liability Directive – withdrawn] Proposal for a Directive on AI liability. COM(2022) 496 final. Status: Withdrawn February 2025 (no consensus among member states). → Liability gap in the AI Act

[OECD AI Definition 2023]

OECD: Recommendation of the Council on Artificial Intelligence. OECD/LEGAL/0449, updated 2023. → Basis for the definition in Art. 3.1 AI Act

[HLEG AI 2019a]

High-Level Expert Group on Artificial Intelligence: *Ethics Guidelines for Trustworthy AI.* European Commission, April 2019. → Foundation for "trustworthy AI," referenced in Recital 27 AI Act

[HLEG AI 2019b]

High-Level Expert Group on Artificial Intelligence: *A Definition of AI: Main Capabilities and Disciplines.* European Commission, April 2019. → Interdisciplinary AI definition

CJEU Case Law

[CJEU C-634/21]

CJEU, Judgment of 7.12.2023 – C-634/21 (OQ v. Land Hessen and Schufa). → Automated decision-making, Art. 22 GDPR, expansion of scope

[CJEU C-579/21]

CJEU, Judgment of 22.6.2023 – C-579/21 (Pankki S). → Interpretation of

Union law: wording, context, purpose

[CJEU C-307/22]

CJEU, Judgment of 26.10.2023 – C-307/22 (DW v. FT). → Recitals are not binding, cannot contradict normative text

German Law

[BGB – Digital Products]

§§ 327–327u BGB (Contracts for digital products). In force since: January 1, 2022. → Digital content and services, update obligation, reversal of burden of proof

3. Standards and Norms

[ISO/IEC 22989:2022]

ISO/IEC 22989:2022: *Information technology – Artificial intelligence – Artificial intelligence concepts and terminology.* International Organization for Standardization, 2022. → Precise technical definition of "AI System," recommended by [Hense/Mustac 2024]

[ISO 42001:2023]

ISO/IEC 42001:2023: *Information technology – Artificial intelligence – Management system.* International Organization for Standardization, 2023. → AI Management System, risk management framework

[ISO 27001]

ISO/IEC 27001:2022: *Information security, cybersecurity and privacy protection – Information security management systems – Requirements.* → Reference for ISMS integration

4. Secondary Literature / Commentaries

[Hense/Mustac 2024]

Hense, Peter; Mustac, Tea: *AI Act kompakt: Compliance, Management & Use Cases in der Unternehmenspraxis.* InTeR-Schriftenreihe. Fachmedien Recht und Wirtschaft, 2024. ISBN 978-3-8005-1823-4 → Provider vs. deployer, risk management, Art. 14–15

[Bock 2025]

Bock, Mario: "Wie denkt und spricht eine KI? – Eine Einführung in Large Language Models." In: *Im Zeitalter der KI: Zwischen Halbwissen und (un)berechtigten Ängsten.* Springer Vieweg, Wiesbaden 2025. DOI: 10.1007/978-3-658-47651-9_3 → Brief LLM introduction

5. Industry Studies and Market Research

[Forrester 2025]

Forrester Research, Inc.: *2026 Predictions: B2B Marketing, Sales, & Product.* Forrester Research, 2025. → Forecast: $10+ billion in damages from ungoverned GenAI; renaissance of human expertise for validation

[Standish CHAOS]

Standish Group: *CHAOS Report.* Annual survey since 1994. → IT project success rates: 16.2% successful, 9% for large enterprises

[Pegasystems 2025]

Pegasystems/Savanta: *Global Enterprise IT Efficiency Study.* 2025. 500+ IT decision-makers worldwide. → $370 million average technical debt damage per year per enterprise

6. Online Resources

[Google ML Crash Course]

Google Developers: *Machine Learning Crash Course.* https://developers.google.com/machine-learning Retrieved: January 2026. → Free introduction, practice-oriented

[Red Hat LLM Guide]

Red Hat: *What Are Large Language Models (LLM)?* https://www.redhat.com/en/topics/ai/what-are-large-language-models Retrieved: January 2026. → Technical overview

7. Black-Box Problem and Explainability

[Rudin 2019]

Rudin, Cynthia: *Stop Explaining Black Box Machine Learning Models for High Stakes Decisions and Use Interpretable Models Instead.* Nature Machine Intelligence 1, 2019, pp. 206–215. PMC9122117 → Fundamental critique: No black-box models for critical decisions

[Ali et al. 2023]

Ali, Sajid et al.: *Interpreting Black-Box Models: A Review on Explainable Artificial Intelligence.* Cognitive Computation, August 2023. DOI: 10.1007/s12559-023-10179-8 → Comprehensive overview of XAI methods, 718 studies analyzed

8. Critique of the Neuron Analogy

[MIT/Khona 2022] Khona, Mikail et al.: *No free lunch from deep learning in neuroscience: A case study through models of the entorhinal-hippocampal circuit.* MIT, November 2022. https://news.mit.edu/2022/neural-networks-brain-function-1102 → Neural networks show brain-like behavior only with artificial constraints

[Quanta 2025] Wolchover, Natalie: *AI Is Nothing Like a Brain, and That's OK.* Quanta Magazine, April 2025. https://www.quantamagazine.org/ai-is-nothing-like-a-brain-and-thats-ok-20250430/ → Artificial neurons are "caricatures" of biological neurons

[Shen 2023] Shen, Zhongzhi: *How can artificial neural networks approximate the brain?* Frontiers in Psychology 14, January 2023. PMC9868316 → Core concepts of ANNs originate from mathematics, not neuroscience

[Hasson et al. 2020] Hasson, Uri; Nastase, Samuel A.; Goldstein, Ariel: *Direct fit to nature: an evolutionary perspective on biological (and artificial) neural networks.* Neuron 105(3), February 2020, pp. 416–434. PMC7096172 → ANNs are extreme abstractions of biological networks

[Stanford/Smith 2010] Smith, Stephen et al.: *New imaging method developed at Stanford reveals stunning details of brain connections.* Stanford Medicine News, November 2010. https://med.stanford.edu/news/all-news/2010/11/new-imaging-method-developed-at-stanford-reveals-stunning-details-of-brain-connections.html → 125 trillion synapses in the cerebral cortex, each synapse like a microprocessor with ~1,000 switches

Citation Format

This book uses short citations in the text: [Ertel 2025, p. 47] [AI Act 2024, Art. 14] [Schmid 2026, Ch. 5] [Forrester 2025]

Last updated: January 2026

Appendix

Template SLA for LLM-Based Services

This template serves as a starting point for contract negotiations. It does not replace legal advice.

1. Subject of Service

The provider makes available to the customer a system for AI-assisted document analysis. The system enables:

- Searching documents according to defined criteria
- Creating summaries
- Identifying potential connections and contradictions

The system is based on Large Language Models (LLMs) that produce stochastic outputs. The system's outputs are to be understood as suggestions that require professional verification by the customer.

2. Availability

2.1 Service Level

Parameter	Target Value	Measurement
System availability	99.5% per month	Monitoring system
API availability	99.9% per month	Health checks
Planned maintenance	Max. 4 hours/month	Advance notice 7 days
Max. downtime	4 hours continuous	Incident tickets

2.2 Measurement Method

Availability is measured as:

Availability = (Total Time - Downtime - Planned Maintenance) / (Total Time - Planned Maintenance) × 100%

Downtime begins with notification by the customer or detection by the monitoring system, whichever occurs first.

2.3 Service Credits

Service credits are granted upon request by the customer. The request must be submitted within 30 days after the end of the affected month.

Availability	Service Credit
< 99.5%	10% of monthly fee
< 99.0%	25% of monthly fee
< 95.0%	50% of monthly fee
< 90.0%	Right to extraordinary termination

3. Response Times

3.1 API Latency

Parameter	Target Value
Median (P50)	< 1 second
95th percentile (P95)	< 3 seconds
99th percentile (P99)	< 10 seconds

3.2 Support Response Times

Prio	Definition	Response Time	Resolution Time
Critical	System unusable	30 minutes	4 hours
High	Function significantly impaired	2 hours	8 hours
Normal	Question, request, partial function	8 business hours	3 business days
Low	Wish, suggestion	2 business days	By agreement

Business hours: Monday–Friday, 8:00 AM–6:00 PM (excluding public holidays at the provider's location).

4. Data Protection and Security

4.1 Data Processing

Parameter	Commitment
Data location	Exclusively EU (Germany, Netherlands, Ireland)
Encryption (transport)	TLS 1.3
Encryption (storage)	AES-256
Retention	Deletion 30 days after contract termination

4.2 Subcontractors

The provider uses the following subcontractors:

[List of subcontractors with function and location]

Changes will be communicated to the customer 30 days before taking effect. The customer may object within 14 days in the event of material changes.

4.3 US Jurisdiction

☐ The provider confirms that no companies in the processing chain are subject to US jurisdiction.

☐ The provider notes that the following companies in the chain are subject to US jurisdiction: [List]

4.4 Audit Rights

The customer has the right to conduct or commission an audit once per year. The provider shall make the required documentation available. Costs are borne by the customer, unless violations are found.

5. Warranty

5.1 The Provider Warrants:

- Technical availability of the system in accordance with the agreed SLAs
- Compliance with the agreed data protection standards
- Provision of support in accordance with the agreed response times
- Documentation of the system and its interfaces

5.2 The Provider Does Not Warrant:

- The substantive correctness of system outputs
- The completeness of search results
- The suitability of outputs for specific purposes
- Freedom from errors, omissions, or inaccuracies
- Consistency of outputs upon repeated queries

Clarification: The system produces stochastic outputs based on statistical patterns. The outputs may be factually incorrect, incomplete, or misleading without any technical defect being present. The customer is responsible for verifying and validating all outputs before use.

6. Customer Obligations

The customer commits to:

- Verifying all system outputs through qualified personnel before use
- Establishing and documenting processes for validation and approval of system outputs
- Ensuring AI competence of its employees in accordance with Art. 4 AI Act
- Informing the provider without delay about systematic errors
- Restricting use of the system to the agreed purposes
- Keeping access credentials confidential and preventing misuse

7. Model Versions

7.1 Planned Changes

The provider shall inform the customer at least 30 days before a planned model version change. The information shall include:

- Designation of the new version
- Material changes
- Possible effects on existing prompts/workflows

The customer has the right to continue using the existing version for an additional 90 days to conduct its own tests.

7.2 Unplanned Changes

In the event of unplanned model version changes by the upstream provider, the provider shall inform the customer without delay and, where possible, make the previous version available for a transition period of at least 30 days.

7.3 Version Pinning

☐ The customer requests version pinning (fixed model version). Surcharge: ______ €/month.

8. Liability

8.1 Unlimited Liability

The provider is liable without limitation for:

- Damages resulting from injury to life, body, or health
- Damages caused intentionally or through gross negligence
- Fraudulent concealment of defects

8.2 Limited Liability

For damages resulting from the use of system outputs, the provider is liable only in cases of intent or gross negligence and only up to the amount of the compensation paid by the customer in the relevant contract year.

8.3 Exclusion of Liability

The provider is not liable for damages arising because the customer:

- Used system outputs without adequate verification
- Failed to fulfill the agreed customer obligations
- Used the system for purposes not covered by the agreement

9. Contract Term and Termination

9.1 Term

The contract begins on ___________ and runs for an indefinite period.

9.2 Ordinary Termination

The contract may be terminated by either party with 3 months' notice to the end of a month.

9.3 Extraordinary Termination

The customer may terminate the contract without notice if:

- Availability falls below 95% in three consecutive months
- The provider materially breaches data protection commitments
- The provider increases prices by more than 20%

9.4 Data Return

Upon contract termination, the provider shall make all data submitted by the customer available in a standard format. The return shall take place within 30 days after contract termination.

10. Final Provisions

10.1 Written Form

Amendments and additions to this contract require written form.

10.2 Applicable Law

The law of the Federal Republic of Germany shall apply.

10.3 Place of Jurisdiction

The place of jurisdiction is ___________.

Signatures

Provider	Customer
Place, date:	Place, date:
Signature:	Signature:
Name:	Name:
Position:	Position:

Note: This template is a working aid and does not replace legal advice. The specific provisions must be adapted to the individual case.

Checklist: AI Introduction in Regulated Industries

This checklist summarizes the requirements from Chapters 9, 10, 11, 13, and 16.

Phase 1: Before the Decision

Problem Definition

☐ Concrete problem defined (not "introduce AI" but e.g. "find latency contradictions in specifications")
☐ Success made measurable (How do we recognize that it works?)
☐ Failure scenario played through (What happens if the system is wrong?)
☐ Consequences of an error documented and accepted

Alternatives

☐ Alternatives without AI seriously evaluated (more personnel, better processes, specialized software)
☐ Decision documented as to why AI was chosen

Provider Selection

☐ Provider promises critically questioned (Red flags: "replaces manual review," "minimized hallucinations," "reliable answers")
☐ Specific model and version known
☐ US jurisdiction clarified (CLOUD Act)
☐ Data location verified

Phase 2: Before Commissioning

Contract

☐ Contract contains clear liability exclusions for substantive correctness
☐ Exclusions understood and communicated internally
☐ Version control regulated (advance notice for model changes)
☐ Exit strategy defined (data return, notice periods)
☐ Audit rights agreed

Compliance

☐ Risk category under AI Act determined
☐ For high risk: Deployer obligations under Art. 26 AI Act known

☐ FRIA required? If yes: conducted
☐ Data protection impact assessment (if personal data involved)

Costs

☐ TCO realistically calculated (not just license costs)
☐ Costs for verification and validation budgeted
☐ Training budget available

Phase 3: Before Go-Live

Competence

☐ Employees named who can professionally evaluate outputs (names, not roles)
☐ Time budget of these employees reserved for verification
☐ Deputization arrangements clarified
☐ Training conducted (Art. 4 AI Act: AI competence)
☐ Training documented

Processes

☐ Process "Use" defined: Who may use the system, for which tasks?
☐ Process "Verification" defined: Who verifies outputs, according to which criteria?
☐ Process "Approval" defined: Who approves decisions?
☐ Process "Escalation" defined: What happens when errors are discovered?
☐ All processes documented

Documentation

☐ Documentation template created (query, output, verification result, decision)
☐ Documentation audit-proof (who, when, what)
☐ Retention periods defined

Technology

☐ Test environment set up
☐ Regression tests defined (known test cases for model changes)
☐ Monitoring set up (availability, latency)

Phase 4: In Operation

Ongoing Verification

☐ Every critical decision based on LLM outputs documented
☐ Errors systematically recorded
☐ Regular reviews of process compliance (monthly/quarterly)
☐ Gradual erosion of verification diligence monitored

Model Changes

☐ Upon announcement of model change: test plan activated
☐ Regression tests conducted
☐ Deviations documented and evaluated
☐ Prompts adjusted as needed
☐ Go/no-go decision documented

Reporting

☐ Management receives honest reports (not just success stories)
☐ Error rates communicated
☐ Effort for validation made transparent

Phase 5: Incident Management

Upon Discovered Error

☐ Immediate documentation (query, output, actual correct value)
☐ Impact analysis (Was the error used in decisions?)
☐ If used: damage mitigation
☐ Root cause analysis (systematic or isolated case?)
☐ For systematic errors: provider informed
☐ Process adjustment as needed

In Case of Damage

☐ Legal advice obtained
☐ Documentation secured
☐ Liability chain analyzed (Who committed to what? Who verified what?)
☐ Insurance notified (if relevant)

Summary: The Critical Questions

Before any AI introduction, these questions should be answerable with "Yes":

- Who can evaluate the outputs? (Concrete names)
- How much time does this person have? (Realistic, not optimistic)
- What happens if the system is wrong? (Played through, not theoretical)
- Is the residual risk accepted? (By management, documented)
- Do we have a Plan B? (If the service fails or becomes unusable)

If any of these questions cannot be answered with "Yes": Not yet ready for productive use.

> This checklist is a working aid. It does not replace legal advice and must be adapted to the specific use case.

Appendix E: How This Book Was Created

E.1 Why This Chapter Exists

Transparency is not weakness. In a book about the limits of AI, it would be dishonest to conceal one's own AI use.

E.2 The Tools

Claude (Anthropic)

- Models: Claude 3.5 Sonnet, Claude Opus 4.5
- Use: Structuring, research, text development, critical discussion
- Access: claude.ai (browser interface)

Additional Tools

- Literature research: Web search, reference books, legal databases
- Word processing: Markdown, later conversion to DOCX
- Version control: Manual backup of work states

E.3 The Process

The chapters were created in dialogue. A typical workflow:

1. **Structuring:** I outlined the topic and argument. Claude proposed outlines.
2. **Research:** Claude searched for sources. I verified and supplemented.
3. **Draft:** Claude formulated text components. I revised.
4. **Critique:** I explicitly asked Claude for contradiction. "What is wrong with my argument?"
5. **Finalization:** I decided what goes into the book.

E.4 What Claude Did Well

- **Structuring:** Organizing complex arguments into logical sections
- **Research:** Finding sources, establishing connections
- **Style review:** Enforcing short sentences, clear language
- **Proofreading:** Identifying inconsistencies and gaps
- **Bibliography:** Systematically building and maintaining

E.5 What Claude Could Not Do

- **Guarantee originality:** Whether an idea is new is something an LLM cannot judge

- **Verify sources:** Claude occasionally "hallucinated" citations. Every source was manually checked.
- **Assume responsibility:** Claude has no legal personality. Errors are my errors.
- **Critical distance:** Claude tends toward agreement. Real criticism had to be demanded.

E.6 The Limits—A Self-Experiment

While working on this book, I experienced multiple times what I was writing about:

- **Session interruptions:** In the middle of work, the session ended. Context was lost.
- **Inconsistent answers:** The same question, different answers.
- **False sources:** Claude occasionally invented bibliographic references. Verification was mandatory.
- **No memory:** Every new session started from zero.

This confirmed my thesis: Such a system is useful as a tool. As a reliable managed service with SLA? Impossible.

E.7 The Ethical Question

Is it legitimate to write an AI-critical book with AI?

I believe: Yes. Under two conditions:

1. **Transparency:** The reader knows how the book was created.
2. **Responsibility:** The author verifies, decides, takes responsibility.

> This book does not argue against AI use. It argues against the illusion that AI can be purchased like a managed service with guaranteed availability and quality.

I used AI. I did not outsource it.

E.8 What Is Not in the Book

The crashes. The lost contexts. The moments when Claude asserted something false with great conviction.

That stays between us.

E.9 Final Remark: Practice, Not Theory

This book recommends the Researcher Model: AI as tool, human as verifier.

The English translation follows this principle. Claude translated the text. I directed, decided, took responsibility. But I am not a native speaker—I cannot conclusively judge the tonality.

So I purchased validation: A Canadian editor with a German background reviews language, style, and natural flow. Proofreading and editing by a human who can do what I cannot.

That costs money. That costs time. That is inconvenient.

But that is exactly the message of this book: Those who cannot verify themselves need someone who can. Anything else would be trust without validation—the Little Helper Paradox in its purest form.

Appendix F: GPU Infrastructure Planning Guide

Who This Appendix Is For

This appendix is aimed at decision-makers considering local LLM systems. It provides planning figures—not deterrence.

The figures are high. That is not an argument against AI. It is an argument for realistic planning.

F.1 Two Architecture Classes

For local LLM systems, there are two fundamentally different hardware approaches.

HGX Platform (High-End)

NVIDIA HGX servers are specialized machines for maximum AI performance. 4–8 GPUs operate as a coherent system via NVLink/NVSwitch. Communication between GPUs is extremely fast.

Optimized for:

- Training large models (>70B parameters)
- Workloads with intensive GPU-to-GPU communication
- Research and development of new models

Not optimized for:

- High availability
- Cost efficiency at partial load
- Simple operation

PCIe GPU Server (Standard)

Classic rack servers with 2–8 GPUs via PCIe bus. The GPUs operate more independently. Bandwidth between GPUs is lower.

Optimized for:

- Inference (production operation)
- Many parallel, independent queries
- Fine-tuning smaller models (<30B parameters)
- Cost efficiency under variable load

Not optimized for:

- Training very large models
- Workloads that distribute GPU memory across multiple cards

F.2 Investment Costs (CAPEX)

The following figures are indicative values for 2025/2026. GPU prices fluctuate significantly.

HGX System (8 GPUs)

Component	Cost
Server with 8× GPU, CPUs, RAM, NVSwitch	€350,000–500,000
High-performance network (InfiniBand/Ethernet)	€20,000–50,000
Storage share (NVMe, shared storage)	€20,000–60,000
Installation and commissioning	€5,000–20,000
Total per node	**€400,000–600,000**

PCIe GPU Server (8 GPUs)

Component	Cost
Server with 8× GPU, standard configuration	€150,000–250,000
Network (standard Ethernet)	€5,000–15,000
Storage share	€15,000–35,000
Installation	€5,000–10,000
Total per node	**€180,000–300,000**

Factor: HGX costs approximately two to three times as much as a PCIe system.

F.3 Operating Costs (OPEX)

Per node and year

Cost Category	HGX	PCIe
Power (4–6 kW, 24/7)	€5,000–15,000	€4,000–10,000
Cooling, rack, UPS	€5,000–20,000	€3,000–12,000
Hardware support (~5% CAPEX)	€15,000–30,000	€8,000–15,000
Software stack (OS, AI frameworks)	€5,000–40,000	€5,000–20,000
Total per year	**€30,000–90,000**	**€20,000–55,000**

Not included: Personnel for operations and maintenance. These costs are organization-dependent and addressed in Chapter 2.3.

F.4 The Redundancy Problem

What HGX Servers Do Not Provide

A single HGX server has the following redundant components:

- Power supplies (N+1)
- Fans
- Network ports

A single HGX server has no redundancy for:

- GPUs
- NVSwitch / NVLink fabric
- Mainboard
- CPU

Consequence: A chassis failure leads to complete workload interruption. There is no uninterrupted continued operation.

This is not a defect. This is the design. HGX maximizes computing power, not availability.

Redundancy Through Architecture

Those who need high availability need multiple systems. There is no other way.

Minimal redundancy:

- 2× HGX server
- Shared storage

- Orchestration (Kubernetes, SLURM)
- CAPEX: €800,000–1,200,000

Production cluster:

- 4–8× HGX server
- Redundant networks
- Separate control plane
- CAPEX: €1,600,000–4,800,000

F.5 Checkpoint Architecture with SAN

The redundancy costs can be limited through intelligent architecture. The key lies not in hardware redundancy but in data redundancy.

The Principle

GPU workloads are stateful. A running training has a state—the current model weights, the optimizer state, the position in the dataset.

This state can be regularly saved to storage: checkpointing.

In the event of a hardware failure, not all work is lost. Training resumes on another node from the last checkpoint.

Architecture Components

Component	Function
SAN (Storage Area Network)	Central, redundant storage for checkpoints
NVMe tier	Fast intermediate storage on each node
Checkpoint interval	Typical: every 15–60 minutes
Orchestration	Automatic restart on available node

Cost-Benefit

Approach	CAPEX	Data Loss on Failure
No checkpoint	€400,000–600,000	Complete
Checkpoint on local storage	+€20,000	Since last local checkpoint
Checkpoint on redundant SAN	+€80,000–150,000	Since last SAN checkpoint
Second HGX system (hot standby)	+€400,000–600,000	Minimal

Recommendation: For most use cases, checkpoint on SAN is the most economically sensible compromise.

What Checkpointing Does Not Solve

- Inference outages: Production API queries need immediate responses. Checkpointing does not help here.
- Latency-critical applications: A restart takes minutes, not milliseconds.

For inference, the answer remains: Multiple systems in active/active operation with load balancer.

F.6 TCO Calculation (5 Years)

Scenario A: Minimal (Training, tolerates outages)

Item	Cost
1× HGX server	€500,000
SAN for checkpoints	€100,000
OPEX (5 years × €60,000)	€300,000
TCO 5 years	**€900,000**

Scenario B: Redundant (Training + Inference)

Item	Cost
2× HGX server	€1,000,000
SAN for checkpoints	€150,000
OPEX (5 years × €120,000)	€600,000
TCO 5 years	**€1,750,000**

Scenario C: Production Cluster

Item	Cost
4× HGX server	€2,000,000
Redundant SAN	€250,000
Network infrastructure	€100,000
OPEX (5 years × €240,000)	€1,200,000
TCO 5 years	**€3,550,000**

F.7 When Does On-Premises Pay Off?

The Break-Even Question

Cloud GPU instances cost approximately €2–4 per GPU hour (H100 class, as of 2025).

On-premises pays off when utilization is high enough:

Utilization	GPU Hours/Month	Recommendation
< 2,000 h	Sporadic	Cloud
2,000–8,000 h	Medium	Hybrid or cloud
> 8,000 h	Sustained load	On-premises

Rule of thumb: From 8,000–10,000 GPU hours per month over several years, on-premises is more economical.

This corresponds to approximately 11–14 hours of GPU usage per day with an 8-GPU system. Those who do not achieve this utilization pay less in the cloud.

F.8 Decision Matrix

Criterion	HGX	PCIe	Cloud
CAPEX	Very high	High	Low
OPEX at sustained load	Medium	Medium	Very high
OPEX at partial load	High (fixed costs)	Medium	Low
Training performance (large models)	Excellent	Limited	Excellent
Inference efficiency	Good	Very good	Good
Availability (single node)	Low	Medium	High
Data sovereignty	Complete	Complete	Limited
Vendor lock-in	High (NVIDIA)	Medium	High (cloud provider)
Time-to-compute	Weeks–months	Weeks	Minutes

F.9 What This Means for Mid-Sized Companies

The figures are clear: GPU infrastructure for production LLM systems starts at just under one million euros TCO over five years. For redundant operation, this amount doubles.

For a company with €50 million in revenue, €350,000 per year (Scenario B) is 0.7% of revenue—for GPU infrastructure alone. Personnel, software, and compliance are additional.

This is not feasible for many mid-sized companies.

The Competitive Distortion

This cost structure creates a structural disadvantage for mid-sized companies versus large corporations.

Company Size	Revenue	AI Infrastructure (€350k/year)	Share of Revenue
Large corporation	€5 billion	Affordable	0.007%
Large mid-sized company	€500 million	Borderline	0.07%
Typical mid-sized company	€50 million	Barely feasible	0.7%
Small company	€10 million	Not feasible	3.5%

The large corporation invests the same absolute amount—but barely feels it. The mid-sized company must manage the same technology with a fraction of the resources.

The result: Corporations build AI competence. Mid-sized companies become consumers of AI services whose quality they cannot evaluate (see Chapter 7).

This is not market dynamics. This is competitive distortion through fixed costs.

The costs for GPU hardware, electricity, and skilled personnel are largely independent of company size. A mid-sized company needs the same hardware for the same application as a corporation. But it has one-tenth of the budget.

Without countermeasures, a two-class economy emerges:

- Companies that can operate and validate AI systems themselves
- Companies that must accept AI results without verification

The first group makes better decisions. The second group bears higher risks with less control.

Possible Paths

Path 1: Forgo Self-Operation

Use managed services, build validation competence internally. The book shows why this is problematic for critical applications.

Path 2: Shared Infrastructure

Multiple companies share GPU clusters. This works when:

- Data remains separated (multi-tenancy)
- Utilization patterns complement each other (different usage times)
- A neutral operator exists

Data centers and universities are increasingly offering such models.

Path 3: Funding Programs

The European Union and the German federal government have defined AI sovereignty as a strategic goal. The infrastructure costs show: Without funding, this sovereignty remains reserved for large enterprises.

Specific starting points for funding programs:

Funding Area	Impact
CAPEX subsidies for GPU hardware	Lowers entry barrier
Operation of regional GPU clusters	Enables shared use
Electricity cost subsidies for AI operation	Reduces OPEX
Training funding for ML-Ops	Addresses skills shortage

The question is not whether AI is economical. The question is who can afford it.

F.10 Summary

- HGX systems deliver maximum training performance but no redundancy by design. CAPEX: €400,000–600,000 per node.
- PCIe GPU servers are more economical and more robust but unsuitable for very large models. CAPEX: €180,000–300,000 per node.
- Redundancy is achieved through multiple systems or through checkpoint architecture with SAN. Both cost money.
- TCO over 5 years: €900,000 (minimal) to €3,550,000 (production cluster).
- Break-even on-prem vs. cloud: From 8,000–10,000 GPU hours per month.
- For mid-sized companies, shared infrastructures and funding programs are decisive.

Checklist: Before the Investment Decision

☐ Is the use case clearly defined? (Training vs. inference vs. both)
☐ How high is the expected utilization? (GPU hours per month)
☐ What availability requirements exist?
☐ Is the data center suitable for GPU systems? (Power, cooling)
☐ What personnel are available for operations?
☐ Have cloud alternatives been calculated?
☐ Are funding opportunities available? (Federal, state, EU)
☐ Is an exit strategy defined? (What happens with technology change?)

The figures in this appendix are indicative values. Specific offers may differ significantly. As of: January 2026.

About the Author

Michael Schmid is a physicist who has worked as an interim manager in critical infrastructures for 28 years. He is the owner of it-dialog e.K. (Stuttgart), which he founded in 2000.

The Path

In 1975, Schmid completed a journeyman's examination in telecommunications engineering with the German Armed Forces—long-distance communication, carrier frequency, digital transmission. In the process, he discovered that he had to explain to engineers how radio communications actually work.

The consequence: he studied physics education at the University of Freiburg—to truly understand the fundamentals and learn to explain them. In 1982, he programmed an ELIZA-like dialogue system—long before the term "chatbot" existed. The experience of how easily people attribute human qualities to a machine shapes his perspective on today's AI discussion.

In 1985, he joined kühn & weyh Software GmbH. There he developed M/OMS—an output management system for mass output and document design for manuals, invoices, contracts, and customer communications. Cincom Systems (Cincinnati, OH) distributed the kühn & weyh software worldwide. The system has been running for 39 years without fundamental redesign. During this time, he built a team of 40 developers.

In 1996, he became self-employed. Since then, he has worked as an interim manager at the junctures where technology and organization collide.

Career Stations

BTC AG, Oldenburg (2005): Interim manager in the "System Management" division—a subsidiary of the fifth-largest German energy provider. Multi-project management with over 20 parallel, mostly complex projects. Building a team of service managers, coaching project leads.
Deutsche Telekom (2005–2008): Migration of the core network—160 million connections in three years.
CIBER: Stabilization of 120 SAP systems with a minimal team. Turnaround through focus.

EWE, Oldenburg: Architecture and project management for the managed service of the transport network control center—power, gas, and water. Critical infrastructure in its purest form.
Critical infrastructure environment: Additional projects for network operators (EWE), energy providers (eprimo/E.ON), and companies in the telecommunications, energy, and defense sectors.

Approach

Schmid's core competence is finding gaps—between what technology promises and what organizations actually need. His credo: After the mandate ends, the competence stays in-house.

This gap-finding led directly to this book. When the LLM wave began in 2023, Schmid observed the daily promises on LinkedIn: "AI-powered quality assurance," "intelligent document analysis," "managed AI services." He asked himself: What does the contract say? Who is liable when things go wrong? The answers—or rather their absence—are the result of this analysis.

Publications

- *Managed Services richtig verstehen* (Understanding Managed Services, 2026)
- *Das Helferlein-Paradox* (The Little Helper Paradox, 2026)
- *Greenfield—Über parallele Neuentwicklung statt Transformation* (Greenfield—On Parallel New Development Instead of Transformation)
- *Verrat im Hotel der Innovation* (Betrayal at the Hotel of Innovation)—A crime novel exploring ideas that Schmid developed while conceiving Germany's first private innovation cluster in 2013

Contact

it-dialog e.K.
Stuttgart
www.it-dialog.com
verlag@it-dialog.com

www.ingramcontent.com/pod-product-compliance
Lightning Source LLC
Chambersburg PA
CBHW050525240926
51846CB00003B/697
9783964590312